RAISING OTHER PEOPLE'S KIDS

About the Authors

M. C. Camerer received the Doctor of Education degree in Curriculum and Instruction from the University of Arkansas. She earned the Bachelor of Education and Master of Special Education degrees from Eastern New Mexico University. She has been a housemother and public school teacher. She is currently an assistant professor in the Gordon T. and Ellen West Division of Education at Midwestern State University in Wichita Falls, Texas.

Emerson Capps received the Master of Education and Doctor of Education degrees in counselor education from the University of Arkansas. He earned his undergraduate degree in education from Northeastern State University in Tahlequah, Oklahoma. He has been a public school teacher and counselor. He is a Licensed Professional Counselor in Texas, a National Certified Counselor, and a trained mediator. Dr. Capps is Director of the Gordon T. and Ellen West Division of Education at Midwestern State University in Wichita Falls, Texas.

RAISING OTHER PEOPLE'S KIDS
A Guide for Houseparents, Foster Parents, and Direct Care Staff

By

M. C. CAMERER, ED.D.

and

EMERSON CAPPS, ED.D.

CHARLES C THOMAS • PUBLISHER
Springfield • Illinois • U.S.A.

Published and Distributed Throughout the World by
CHARLES C THOMAS • PUBLISHER
2600 South First Street
Springfield, Illinois 62794-9265

This book is protected by copyright. No part of
it may be reproduced in any manner without
written permission from the publisher.

© 1995 by CHARLES C THOMAS • PUBLISHER
ISBN 0-398-05985-3 (cloth)
ISBN 0-398-05986-1 (paper)
Library of Congress Catalog Card Number: 94-48371

With THOMAS BOOKS *careful attention is given to all details of manufacturing and design. It is the Publisher's desire to present books that are satisfactory as to their physical qualities and artistic possibilities and appropriate for their particular use.* THOMAS BOOKS *will be true to those laws of quality that assure a good name and good will.*

Printed in the United States of America
SC-R-3

Library of Congress Cataloging-in-Publication Data

Camerer, M. C. Gore
    Raising other people's kids : a guide for houseparents, foster
parents, and direct care staff / by M.C. Camerer and Emerson Capps.
      p.   cm.
    ISBN 0-398-05985-3 (cloth). — ISBN 0-398-05986-1 (pbk.)
    1. Child development. 2. Children—Institutional care. 3. Child
rearing. I. Capps, Emerson. II. Title.
HQ767.9.C353   1995
649'.1—dc20
                                            94-48371
                                              CIP

To Mr. Phillip Wilson, my junior high band director, mentor, and friend, who by the way he loved and disciplined his students, taught me all I'll ever need to know about raising other people's kids.

M. C.

To Rosemary, who taught me about love and raising kids.

E. C.

PREFACE

Raising Other People's Kids: A Guide for Houseparents, Foster Parents, and Direct Care Providers is a down-to-earth, practical guide to child development and interpersonal relationship skills. Theoretical work in child development and interpersonal relationships is translated into plain, everyday language and illustrated by a rich variety of houseparents' and foster parents' personal experiences.

The book covers development of the whole child: intellectual, psychological, and moral development. Specific techniques for creating an environment which nurtures the development of the whole child are offered. The learning theory of Vygotsky is carefully explained to assure that care providers can more effectively teach the children in their care. Particular attention is paid to nurturing moral development in children who may have had little training in ethical behavior.

Drs. Camerer and Capps also address the stresses of living in the fishbowl environment of the group home, and they offer techniques for improving communication skills. Dr. Capps, a trained mediator, explains how care providers can become mediators in order to help residents and colleagues learn conflict resolution skills.

Readers may be particularly interested in the chapter in which the authors report the results of a survey of houseparents across the country. Institution supervisors selected their best houseparents to answer these questions: What is your best piece of advice to other houseparents? And what pitfalls would you warn other houseparents to avoid?

Finally, Dr. Camerer and Dr. Capps outline simple methods of preventing and reducing the stress which shortens the tenure of many direct care providers.

M. C.
E. C.

CONTENTS

		Page
Preface		vii
Chapter		
1.	Introduction	3
2.	How Little Kids Think	5
3.	How Older Kids Think	17
4.	How Kids Think About Right and Wrong	25
5.	Creating a Moral Climate	38
6.	How Kids Develop Psychosocially	45
7.	The Identity Crisis	57
8.	Improving Children's Self-Esteem	66
9.	Motivating Kids to Be Responsible and Have Self-Control	79
10.	How to Teach Kids	95
11.	Disciplining Kids	105
12.	Living in a Fishbowl	117
13.	Communicating Better with Kids and Co-Workers	128
14.	Resolving Conflict for Kids and Co-Workers	142
15.	Advice from Houseparents	155
16.	Handling Stress	166
Index		173

RAISING OTHER PEOPLE'S KIDS

Chapter 1

INTRODUCTION

Standing in the door between the kitchen and the yard, seventeen-year-old Travis raised his BB gun to his shoulder, took aim, and shot the window out of the barn. He looked back at his foster parents and grinned. His foster mother dropped the Blue Willow dish she was washing. It shattered on the floor.

I know. I was there. I was his foster mother.

Although I have been a housemother, a foster mother, and a school teacher, kids still find ways to leave me feeling like Elmer Fudd when Buggs Bunny has once again dumbfounded him. I've taught elementary school, junior high school, and high school and I still haven't learned all the tricks. But I have learned some of them, and this book shares the answers to those tricks that I have learned.

Some of the answers came to me through practical experience: I tried this or that and it worked. Many of the answers came to me through my husband. He had spent many years as a policeman and he knew how to handle people (particularly teenage boys) more skillfully than anyone I have ever met. Still other answers came to me through reading and research. And still others from my colleagues, such as Dr. Emerson Capps, who has co-authored this book.

Before we begin to get into the nuts and bolts of discussing the business of raising other people's kids, however, I want to answer some questions that you may be asking.

First: No, houseparenting and fosterparenting weren't what I thought they were going to be either.

Second: Yes, I did want to run away and hide seventeen times a day.

Third: Yes, I was amazed by the paperwork and the bureaucracy.

Fourth: Yes, it was my absolute faith in the belief that I had been called by a higher power to serve in this way that kept me sane.

Fifth: No, I never killed any of my kids and buried them down by the creek.

As you read this book, I urge you to read interactively. By that, I mean that as you read, read slowly and *really think* about what you're reading. When you read a section, stop and recall a similar incident in your experience. Think about the similarities and differences between the two incidents. Discuss it with your colleagues.

Take lots of notes in the margins of this book. It will help you to remember important points and help you to find information again if you want to refer to it later.

As you read and think, devise plans for future action. For example, tell yourself, "Okay, I just read about a particular technique for resolving conflict. Next time that Teresa and Lonnie get into an argument, then I am going to do such and such."

Before we go on, let me explain who is speaking when in this book. You will find that sometimes a passage is worded, "*We say* thus and so." Sometimes a passage is worded, "*I did* thus and so." When we use "we say," it means that both authors agree with a perspective or a statement. When we use "I did," it will usually be me (M. C. Camerer) speaking about a houseparenting experience that I have had. However, in Chapter 14, "I" refers to Emerson Capps, who is a trained mediator. In this chapter, he will be talking about specific mediation experiences that he has had. But just roll with the flow and don't worry about who is speaking when.

One final thought: When you are (1) washing the sheets that Alyson threw up on last night, (2) Tory has just told you to drop dead because you aren't his mom/dad and you can't tell him what to do, and (3) your senior houseparent griped you out for letting the kids raid the refrigerator before bedtime, know that you are not alone and unappreciated.

How can I say that? Because the co-authors of this book go to bed every night and thank God that there are people like you out there, devoting their lives to the high calling of raising other people's kids.

Chapter 2

HOW LITTLE KIDS THINK

The most embarrassed I ever was in college was over a Swiss guy named Jean Piaget. He wasn't in my child and adolescent psychology class; he was a guy we *read about* in my child and adolescent psychology class. His first name is pronounced *Zh-ah-n,* with the J sounding like the J in Jacques Cousteau's name. His last name is pronounced *Pee-ah-zhay,* with the g sounding like the J in Jacques Cousteau's name.

My professor, Dr. Natividad Mascarenas, asked me to stand up and read aloud out of our book. Never before or since have I ever been asked to stand up and read aloud in a college class. I don't know whether that's because it's really rare for college students to have to do that or whether it's because my reputation for being a dunce preceded me. Either way, here's what happened.

Dr. Allen asked me to stand up and read aloud. Now, we'd been talking about Piaget for quite some time, so the entire class knew what his name was, but when I came to it, I blanked out for a second and pronounced it exactly like it looks: Jean Piaget. All hundred or so people in that class busted a gut laughing, and I wanted to crawl out the door and never be seen again.

So much for that. In spite of our poor start together, I became interested in Jean Piaget the man and in his work on kids.

Piaget was a Swiss scientist who was one of those one in a zillion geniuses. When he was only twelve years old, he had an article published in a prestigious scientific journal. He was a bird-watcher, and he had spied a bird in the park near his home that was rare and never before reported in his geographic area. The publication of his article won him fame throughout the scientific community, and the scientific community nodded its gray head and eagerly anticipated hearing from the child prodigy again.

When Piaget was completing the doctorate degree at a rather young age, he wrote his doctoral dissertation on a certain species of mollusk.

Now, following slugs along while they're slugging around is not my idea of a good time, but Piaget got off on it. However, after he completed his doctoral dissertation and degree, Piaget forgot all about mollusks and turned his attention elsewhere.

His wife was about to have their first baby, and Piaget was tickled pink. This was in the 1920s, long before men were taking an active role in childrearing, so his great interest in the coming birth made him famous in the neighborhood. When the baby was finally born, Piaget stopped all of his scientific studies at the university and began to spend day and night watching his new baby. The women in the neighborhood were envious of Mrs. Piaget, to have a husband who so doted upon their child. Then men in the neighborhood hated him, because their wives kept saying, "Why don't you take time with our children like that lovely Dr. Piaget does with his child?"

While at first Mrs. Piaget was pleased, I doubt that she stayed pleased for long, because watching that baby became Piaget's obsession. At first he merely watched the baby. Then he took notes on everything it did. Then he tied a string around its foot which he attached to a bell hanging over the crib. He studied its responses to the contraption and was delighted when the baby seemed to finally make a connection between shaking its leg and making the bell ring. Piaget devised one little experiment after another to see what the child would do. He continued on spending at least eight hours a day watching and taking notes on the baby until the next child was born. Now, whether or not he actually participated in the child's care, no one seems to know. But I'll lay my money on odds that whenever the baby filled its diaper, Piaget hollered, "Honey! The baby needs you!"

The birth of each of Piaget's next two children brought him more subjects to study. The three children were his sole scientific subjects for many years. He carefully catalogued who did what at exactly when. What he found was that the children seemed to share milestones in intellectual development. For example, they seemed to each discover at the same time the connection between shaking the leg to which the string was tied and the ringing of the bell.

Piaget was convinced that born into each child was a genetic time clock that governed when a child would become capable of learning new sorts of things. The milestones governed by this genetic clock occurred in an orderly manner in the same way that a baby's ability to sit up always precedes its ability to stand up. Piaget called this notion epigenesis, which means that the abilities are inborn and occur in an orderly manner. He also explained that the specific things that a baby learned were dependent on her interaction with a specific environment.

Piaget's work was read with great interest in the scientific community and he soon had students working with him to extend his studies to children in countries all over the world. Piaget's theory of epigenesis seemed to be confirmed as he and his students tested thousands of other children.

Piaget's theory provides an important foundation for everything childcare workers do every day. An incredible amount of child psychology and child development is founded on his work, so it is important that a houseparent or foster parent pay careful attention and spend time thinking reflectively on his work.

Piaget described four major stages of intellectual development: *sensorimotor, preoperational thought, concrete operational thought,* and *formal operational (or abstract) thought.* It is important to note that we don't stop using one type of thought simply because we have developed a new type of thought. Instead, we add the new way of thinking to our old ways of thinking. Piaget describes it like building a pyramid. The new thinking skills are added to the old ones. In this chapter, we will discuss the sensorimotor and preoperational stages. In the next chapter, we will discuss the concrete and formal operational stages.

Piaget's sensorimotor stage normally spans birth to two years of age. Preoperational thought is added at about two years of age. Concrete operational thought begins at about seven years, and formal operations begins at eleven years of age.

Piaget found that his babies all seemed to be born with certain reflexes. The reflexes seemed to be a survival mechanism. The babies had an instinct to suck and an instinct to grasp with their hands. These instincts to interact with the environment (suck on things and grasp things) are vital for babies to begin learning about their world. For example, it isn't long before a baby who has an instinct to suck learns to root about and find his mother's nipple. In fact, if the nipple touches his cheek, the baby quickly learns to turn his head toward the nipple. When you think about it, that's a pretty impressive piece of behavior for a week-old baby.

The sensorimotor stage is the stage in which a baby gains knowledge of the world through physical experiences. She experiences her world through physical movement (hence motor) and through her vision, hearing, taste, smell, and touch (hence sensory). The sensorimotor stage includes two important hallmarks for people raising other people's children: *object permanence* and *imitation.* Object permanence means that the child understands that something still exists even though she can't see it any more. We've all played peekaboo with a baby. Suppose we are playing peekaboo with a baby using a teddy bear. Before the baby (let's call her Tina) has object permanence, when we cover up her teddy bear with a blanket, it no longer exists for her. Tina will turn her interest to the stuffed duck sitting beside her. If Tina can't see the bear, it doesn't exist. When we uncover the bear: Surprise! The bear exists again and Tina beams with pleasure.

Suppose, however, that Tina has developed object permanence. She sees the bear and reaches for it. We cover it up so that she can't see it any more. Tina giggles, reaches for the blanket and pulls on it. She knows that the bear is still there; it's simply hidden. She uncovers the bear: Hooray! She has succeeded in getting her bear back.

The notion of object permanence is extremely important in the development of all children; it may present interesting problems in raising other people's kids. For example, I remember being a tiny little kid when my parents would take me to church. They left me in the nursery and went on into the chapel. I screamed and cried and tried to hang on to them. I didn't know that they would be back. As far as I was concerned, they had ceased to exist. They were off somewhere in the Twilight Zone. Although I never did like staying in the church nursery, once I understood that they would be back, things weren't so bad.

Another example is of a mentally retarded youngster whom I had. Bobby was a high schooler who had been a resident of the state school before he was placed in my classroom. Everyone in town knew Bobby and his family. So frequently, when Bobby and I would be about on the school campus, someone would see us and come up to say hello. The conversations would go something like this:

Stranger: Hi, Bobby!

Bobby: Who are you?

Stranger: I'm a friend of your mother's.

Bobby: No! My mother doesn't know you!

Stranger: (Laughing) Sure, she does. We're in the community choir together!

Bobby: No! My mother doesn't know you! I've never seen you with my mother!

The problem for Bobby was that if he had not actually seen his mother and someone else together, then he could not imagine that such a meeting might have taken place. Only what he directly observed could exist.

It was fun to work with Bobby to try to convince him that things existed even if he did not see them. As he developmentally matured, he began to believe me when a stranger said hello and explained that she knew Bobby's mother or father. I would explain over and over that Bobby's mother and dad went places and did things while Bobby was at school, just as he went places and did things at school that they did not know about. However, if Bobby weren't developmentally ready for this lesson, he would have never believed me.

Now think about this: Here's Tina, and she is beginning to understand object permanence. She has started making the connection between the teddy bear still existing when it is covered up, and Mama still existing when she is out of sight. Tina learns that if she cries, Mama can come pick her up, because Mama still exists. But suppose that one day Mama doesn't come back. Tina is placed in your foster or group home. While Tina may continue to understand object permanence, there may be serious disruptions in her thought, because that most precious of objects, Mama, has not reappeared when beckoned and has, in a sense, ceased to exist.

The second hallmark of Piaget's sensorimotor stage is imitation, or the ability to copy behaviors. Thank heaven for imitation, because it is the vehicle by which we learn to speak. When Tina sees me point to the dog and say, "Dog," she tries to imitate me. She says, "Og," and I can't stop myself from saying, "Yes, it's Dog. Nice Dog." Hearing me say dog again, she again tries to imitate me. I think it's interesting that without thinking about how to teach their children to speak, humans have been doing it for thousands of years. It comes so naturally. In teaching Tina to speak, I've never thought to myself, "Okay, now what will I do to get her to learn to say dog?" Without being able to stop myself, I plunge ahead into an interaction with her which will lead to her learning language through her instinctive imitation and my instinctive modeling of language.

The notion of modelling is important to child care providers, because many children come to us without having had language to imitate. "I can't imagine people who don't talk to their babies," said my friend Paige, who never stopped talking to her babies. But unfortunately, many parents are so consumed by their own problems that there simply isn't enough energy left over to interact with Baby. Tina lies in her crib and stares at the ceiling. Or perhaps she is propped in front of the television set. At least the television set offers her language to listen to, but it doesn't interact with her. Besides, the language flies by so quickly that it's unlikely that she will catch enough of it to imitate. Suppose, however, that she is watching "Sesame Street." A dog is shown and the announcer says "Dog." That's better than nothing (and "Sesame Street" *is* wonderful), but when Tina responds with "Og," no one is present to interact with her by modeling the correct response and extending her language.

Extending is the act of adding more words to a child's response. For example, my saying, "Yes, it's Dog. Nice Dog," extends Tina's speech, because I have added more words to her response. Language specialists tell us that when we extend a baby's speech, we should add only one or two words to her response. I think it's interesting that in the same way that parents have intuitively known that by speaking to their babies the babies will learn language, those same parents have intuitively known how to extend their babies' speech. After all, I've never heard a baby say to her mother, "Dog," and heard the mother reply, "Yes, you are right. It is a dog and it lives with us. It is our family pet and it will be three years old next Friday." No, the mothers I've heard have answered Baby by saying, "Yes, it's Dog. Nice Dog."

When a new baby comes into your home, I can't stress enough how important it is that you hold that baby and talk to her as frequently as she can tolerate the attention. Talk to her about everything. Talk to her when you are changing her. Talk about each step in the changing process. Tell her what you are doing to her ("Now I'm rubbing lotion on your bottom"). Tell her what things feel like ("The lotion feels cold! And it feels smooth!") Talk to her while you are feeding her. Talk about what she is doing and what things taste like. Talk, talk, talk. Give her tubsful of words to imitate. And when she starts talking, talk back to her and extend her speech.

The baby will imitate not only what you say but also what you do. Since babies have an instinctive ability to grasp, move your hand in a grasping motion in front of her. She will imitate the motion. If you peekaboo with her, she will peekaboo back. If you bob your head from right to left, she will bob her head, too. Many of the games that parents and babies play are imitation games. To think that the parents didn't know that they were teaching their babies in the most appropriate way when they were playing with them!

Near the end of the sensorimotor stage, Tina will begin to demonstrate *deferred imitation.* Deferred imitation refers to imitating something that is not currently happening. If Tina imitates her older sister who is practicing a dance routine, she is imitating. But if Tina imitates the dance routine later that evening when her sister is nowhere to be seen, that is deferred imitation. Deferred imitation also refers to Tina's announcing that she is a train and running through the house hollering "Tooot! Toooot!" Or saying that she is a dog and lapping the milk out of her bowl of cereal.

In one of the books in the *Ramona* series by Beverly Cleary, Ramona has a book that she loves. The book is about a steam shovel. Ramona runs around the house making noises like a steam shovel and drives her sister, Beezus, bonkers. Ramona is engaging in deferred imitation. Ramona's deferred imitation results in Beezus's imminent irritation. Nonetheless, deferred imitation is an important milestone in a baby's development at the sensorimotor level.

The second stage that Piaget describes is the preoperational stage. Piaget uses the word operation to refer to actions based on logical thinking. The child's actions at the preoperational stage are based on thought, but the thought is not always logical from an adult's perspective. Since Piaget uses the term operation to refer to behavior based on logical thought, the preoperational stage is characterized by behavior based on a lack of logic.

One type of thought that occurs at the preoperational level is called *magical thinking.* My favorite example of magical thinking is when my husband, Kelvin, goes to the refrigerator, discovers that we are out of milk, and then returns ten minutes later to look inside again. Since he looked in the refrigerator ten minutes earlier, he knows that we have no milk. Yet, he feels compelled to go look again, just in case some milk has appeared by magic.

Kelvin's favorite story of preoperational thought concerns the sixth grade students he used to teach. Each Monday, he posted a computer sheet showing all assignments to date during the quarter, the grade for each assignment, and the resulting average. (Each student had a code number, so no one knew what anyone else's grades were.) The great advantage of this was that students made certain that they made up missed assignments, since they didn't like having a blank grade on their row of grades.

The interesting thing was that when Tina would bring Kelvin her paper, he would look at it and grade it in her presence. Then she would rush to the bulletin board to look at the grade sheet. Since Kelvin had not left school, gone home, recorded the new grade, printed out a new grade sheet, brought back the new grade sheet and posted it, Tina would find that the blank spot still existed on her line. Terribly upset, she would return to Kelvin and announce that she had not received credit for her work.

One of the hallmarks of preoperational thought is *symbolic representation*. Symbolic representation means learning to use things as symbols for other things. For example, when Tina takes her spoon and says that it is a jet plane, she is using symbolic representation. Tina knows that the spoon is not a plane, but she is using it as a symbol of a plane. She might as easily have used the spoon as a symbol for a boat, a dog, or a cigar.

The most important symbol that children learn to use is language, and at this stage, the child's language multiplies by about eight thousand percent. But this is the tricky part. Many parents think that because their child can describe something, she thinks logically about that thing. Tina may be able to use the sound symbols of our language to describe her cat in great detail. She may be able to tell you all about feeding and watering her cat. In spite of the detailed descriptions of cats and cat feeding, Tina does not have the logic to understand that if she doesn't feed and water her cat, it will die.

Houseparents are challenged daily by children who don't have logical thought. One of my thirteen-year-old boys, Devon, did not have concrete thought because he suffered from fetal alcohol syndrome. Devon was not a pyromaniac by any means. He wasn't even particularly interested in fire; however, he often blew out the pilot light on the gas stove, because he didn't understand that it was dangerous. Devon had no desire to hurt anyone. He would never have caused injury to the rest of the family. But he still blew out the pilot light because he didn't have logical thought.

Three other hallmarks of preoperational thought are *perceptual centration, irreversibility,* and *egocentrism*. Perceptual centration is why when a houseparent says to Tina, "I told you to clean up your room. Why didn't you do it?" Tina indignantly barks, "I did so clean up my room! I made my bed!"

Perceptual centration refers to a child's tendency to focus attention on only one part of an object or problem. Children at the preoperational level find it almost impossible to see the entire picture. When the bed is unmade, clothes are strung all over the floor, the remains from a sandwich and an apple grace the dresser top, and a damp bath towel is hanging from the doorknob, Tina only sees the unmade bed. She makes it, and from her perspective, the room is clean.

I remember being five years old when I received one of the rare spankings of my life. It was Saturday morning, and my brother had a guest spend Friday night. They were playing in the back yard, and my father instructed me to go pick up their pajamas where they were abandoned on the vanity in the bathroom. I complained that I should not have to pick up the pajamas because they were not mine, but he insisted. I went and picked up the pajamas and put them in my brother's room. Then I returned to watching Bugs Bunny on TV.

Shortly thereafter, my father came in, grabbed me up, and spanked me. I objected loudly that I hadn't done anything wrong. He insisted that I had disobeyed him. I knew that I had not done any such thing, so you can imagine my astonishment when he marched me into the bathroom and there lay a pajama bottom on the floor. I had picked up the three pieces that lay on the vanity. Due to my perceptual centration, I had not seen the pajama bottoms on the floor.

Piaget discovered perceptual centration by conducting experiments with water glasses and modeling clay. The experiments were called *conservation tasks*. First, he took an eight-ounce glass that was tall and thin. Then he took an eight-ounce glass that was short and squat. He asked a child which glass would hold more. The child responded that the tall glass would hold more. Next, with the child watching, Piaget filled the short, squat glass with water. Then he poured the water from the short glass into the tall, thin one. In spite of seeing him pour one full glass into another glass which was then full, the child maintained that the tall, thin glass held more than the short, squat one did. Pouring the water in the tall glass back into the short glass, Piaget was again told that the short glass held less water. When he asked the child where the extra water went, she didn't know, yet insisted that the tall glass held more. The essence of the problem was that the child centered on the height of the glasses and so was unable to think about the width.

Piaget then showed the child a ball of clay. Next, he rolled the ball out into a long, thin snake. The child insisted that the snake consisted of more clay than the balls consisted of. Although Piaget changed the clay from ball to snake to ball again, the child still maintained that the snake was more clay than the ball was.

I think that perceptual centration may also concern houseparents when children fight over who got the bigger share of cake. We always had snacks after school and before bed, and sometimes I didn't cut the sheet cake squarely. Some of the pieces were longer and skinnier, while others were fatter and shorter. But they all consisted of an almost identical number of grams. Still, the little boys with the short, fat pieces insisted that the little boys with the long, skinny pieces had more cake. You just can't win sometimes.

Irreversibility is another characteristic of the preoperational stage. Irreversibility means the inability to reverse a mental action. It's easiest to explain by saying that a child who knows that $4 + 1 = 5$ will not be able to solve the reverse of the problem $5 - 1 = ?$.

While that's helpful for a direct care provider to know when helping a young child with learning arithmetic, it's more helpful for a direct care provider to know when helping a young child search for a lost pair of shoes.

"I can't go to kindergarten today! I can't find my shoes!" cries Monty three minutes before the bus leaves.

You are frantic. If Monty misses the bus, you have to drive him to kindergarten, and today is wash-the-linens day, so you don't have time to run into town with him.

"Backtrack in your mind," you say. "Where did you leave them?"

Monty looks blank.

"Backtrack! Backtrack! You've got to get your shoes and get on the bus! Start with where you were last and work backward!"

Monty still looks blank.

Sound familiar? Monty's problem is that he can't backtrack in his mind. If you asked him to start with when he came home yesterday, he might be able to tell you in chronological order every place he went. But he can't start with now and backtrack, because he doesn't have reversibility yet.

Egocentricism is an interesting hallmark of preoperational thought. We usually think of the word egocentric as a negative word, but that's not the way that Piaget meant it. When he said that young children are egocentric, he meant that each one believes that she is the center of the universe and that everyone's experience is the same as her own experience. That's the reason that Tina gives her foster mother a dead frog for a present. Tina is unable to think about a gift from her foster mother's perspective. Since Tina would like a dead frog, it never occurs to her that her foster mother might not want one.

Another example of egocentrism is when the Tina tells you what you are doing, as though you weren't aware of it. Little kids sometimes drive me crazy by telling me what I am doing. For example, when I was a teacher, if I were sick and missed a day of school, each little one would come up to me when I returned and told me, "You weren't here yesterday." That was okay for the first fifteen or twenty times, but by the time all thirty-two children had come up and told me that I had been absent, I needed to take another sick day to get over the headache that I had.

There are other behaviors that are attributed to egocentric thought. One of them is *animism*. Animism means attributing life to inanimate objects. My mother understood animism when I was a toddler and fell down and skinned my knee. After she "kissed it to make it well," she took me outside and scolded and spanked the "bad sidewalk" for skinning my knee. Lo, these many years later I still remember those scenes, and how avenged and relieved I felt. A houseparent's few minutes spent in scolding a bad sidewalk could go a long way in making a child feel loved, particularly if it's another person's child who doesn't feel loved to begin with.

Finalism stems from egocentric thought also. Finalism is the belief that all things happen for a reason. That's why little kids ask "Why?" until you want to scream and stick your head in the oven.

Houseparent says, "It's time for bed."
Toddler says, "Why?"
"Because it's late."
"Why?"
"Because it's nine o'clock."
"Why?"
Houseparent loses it and is carted away in a straightjacket.

Another feature of egocentrism is called *collective monologue*. Collective monologue takes place when a group of young children are playing near each other and appear to be having a conversation. But when you listen to them closely, you will see that they are not having a conversation. Each of them is conducting a monologue talking to herself. Imagine Tina, Keisha, and Rowena sitting together in the floor, each dressing up her favorite doll.

Tina says, "I want a peanut butter and jelly sandwich. But I don't like the crunchy kind. It hurts my teeth."

Keisha says, "My doll needs a bath. I need to give my dirty baby a bath."

Rowena says, "Mommy said I can go with her to the grocery store today."

Although it is a behavior characteristic of young children, my husband and I often engage in collective monologue instead of talking to each other. Last week I came home and said to him, "My favorite silk blouse has a stain on it and the dry cleaners couldn't get it out." I wanted him to tell me how sorry he was that my favorite blouse was ruined.

What he said was, "I have to go buy some horse feed."

I said, "Now I don't have anything that goes with my best skirt."

He said, "I think I'll get oats instead of sweetfeed this time."

I dropped down on the couch and held my head in my hands in despair. I said, "I just hate myself for ruining that blouse! I'll never find another one to go with my skirt!"

He said, "Six sacks of oats ought to get me through until payday."

I ran out of the room screaming.

The most direct effect of collective monologue on houseparents is that it makes the houseparent feel as though the young child is not listening to what is being said to her, which is basically true. I hope it at least makes you feel better to understand why this occurs.

Last of all, I want to talk about *immaculate perception*. No, immaculate perception has nothing to do with the Immaculate Conception. Immaculate perception refers to the young child's inability to discriminate between fantasy and reality. It is very much like schizophrenia in adults. For example, I once had Hope, a preoperational child who told me that witches were in the closet. I was never able to convince Hope that nothing but her clothes were in the closet. She didn't believe me, because since she had imagined that they were there, the witches were real to her. I was unable to solve the problem until someone told me about Monster-Away Spray. Monster-Away Spray is water in a squirt bottle. I took a bottle of Monster-Away Spray into Hope's room, sprayed the closet with it, and she went to sleep, satisfied.

In this chapter, we have discussed Jean Piaget and his theory of intellectual or cognitive development. We have looked at the development of the intellect in infants and in young children under the age of seven. In the next chapter, we will examine the intellectual growth of children from the age of seven to twelve, and then the intellectual development of children from the age of twelve to adulthood and beyond.

Chapter 3

HOW OLDER KIDS THINK

In the last chapter, we discussed in some detail Piaget's theory of intellectual development in general and the development of the intellect during infancy and to age six or seven in particular. In this chapter, we will discuss the intellectual development of the seven- to twelve-year-old-child and then the development of the child over twelve years of age.

The amazing hallmark of intellectual development at about six years of age is the ability to use logic. The logic is limited to concrete things that the child can see and touch, but it's logic nonetheless. This new ability to use logic is what Piaget called concrete operational thought.

Before we begin to discuss the development of concrete operational thought, however, we need to discuss another major facet of Piaget's theory, and that consists of three things: *schemata, assimilation* and *accommodation*.

Schemata refers to a person's tendency to organize information in her world. You can think of schemata as a filing cabinet in the brain. The individual folders in the filing cabinet are called schema. Suppose that Tina has a schemata filing cabinet for clothes. Each type of clothing has a folder in her filing cabinet. One file is labeled *pants*, and that file contains all the information that Tina knows about pants. Blue jeans are in there. So are sweat pants. So are pants that have matching blouses. Another file is labeled *tops*. Tee shirts are in this file. So are sweat shirts, silk blouses, and cotton blouses. Tank tops and Oxford shirts are in there. That's the extent of Tina's schemata about clothing.

Tina comes to your group home, and you tell her that she has to put on a dress to go to church on Sunday. Tina has never been to church on Sunday or any other day for that matter, and dresses aren't part of her world. Back at her home, Mama didn't have a dress, and neither did Tina, and although Tina saw ladies on soap operas wear dresses, dresses were no more in her schemata of things to wear than thong bathing suits are in mine. So when you tell Tina to put on her new dress, she refuses.

Now, while it seems perfectly reasonable to you that Tina wear a dress, it seems perverse and unreasonable to Tina. Since she doesn't have a schema (file) in her schemata (file cabinet) for dresses, the only thing that she has to compare them to are tops. And no one in her right mind would wear a top without pants. WHAT IS WRONG WITH YOU THAT YOU WANT HER TO GO OUT IN PUBLIC NOT WEARING ANY PANTS???!!!

This is the same reason that a small child raised in the city will call the first horse or cow that she sees "a dog." She has a schema for dogs and one for cats, and that's it. Therefore, a four-legged animal has to be one or the other. We laugh and help her build a new file for horses or cows and all ends well. But when Tina tells us that she is not about to wear this dress, we find her totally unreasonable, because we have told her to do something and she has refused to comply. What we need to do is realize that she lacks a file for this odd garment and help her build one for it.

As a matter of fact, those of us who were growing up in the sixties remember tunics. They barely covered our private business, so while we put them in our file for dresses, our moms put them in their files for shirts. Our moms simply didn't have a schema for dresses that were so short you couldn't bend over to pick up a dime on the sidewalk. When you come to think of it, a dress actually is a long top, so when we wear dresses, we actually are leaving the house with only our underpants between us and the big, bad world.

My mother often recalls the time when I was three years old and Daddy had to dress me for church because she was sick in bed. She was asleep when we left, so Mama didn't see me until after Daddy and I got home after church. She took one look at me and said to my father, "What in the world were you thinking to let this child wear her pink, frilly dress with long pants, her holey cowboy hat, and her holster and toy guns to church?"

Daddy shrugged and said, "That's what she wanted to wear."

At three, I didn't have a schema for dresses that differed from tops, so wearing pants seemed like the thing to do. Since Mama always put a hat on me when we went to church, I looked in my file marked "hats" and pulled one out. It happened to be my favorite old cowboy hat. Since my cowboy hat was also in my file marked "cowboy stuff," I found my holster and guns beside it and put them on, too.

If schemata is our file cabinet, and schema are our individual files, then assimilation is adding more stuff to our files, and accommodation is changing the stuff that's in our files. Together, assimilation and accommodation are called *adaptation*, and adaptation is what Tina is having to do a passel of when she comes into your home.

Since Tina has a file for tops, when you give her a blouse with ruffles on it, she assimilates the ruffled blouse into her top schema. Ruffles are new to Tina, but she recognizes the blouse as being a top, so her file is fatter, but essentially unchanged as to its structure. Assimilation accounts for the growth of schema, but it doesn't address the issue of change of schema.

When schema change, it is called accommodation. After you spend time talking with Tina about dresses, letting her see you in your dress, and taking her to church where she sees other people wearing their dresses, then her schema undergoes a fundamental change. She may alter her file tops to have one section called *short tops that are worn with pants* and another section called *long tops that are not worn with pants*. She may instead make a whole new file called dresses. Either way, her schemata has undergone a major change. That's accommodation.

A major accommodation that many children in out-of-home placements must make is related to food. In our cottage, new boys would almost always "swipe" food and hide it in their rooms. The notion of swiping food wasn't in our schema, because we wanted every child to have all the food he wanted. But since the boys had often come from homes where there wasn't enough food, the notion of taking a second piece of fruit or a leftover piece of cake was "swiping" food in their food schema. Only as boys began to learn that abundant food would always be available would they stop hoarding.

Another accommodation of food schema is related to the types of food that a child has in her schema. Many children come to placement having lived primarily on potato chips, soft drinks, candy, and pizza. This is not to imply that pizza is a junk food, because I don't think it is. I am simply saying that pizza is a food that the children who came into our home had often eaten as staple fare. When the child is given nutritionally balanced meals for the first time, she may reject the new foods because they aren't in her schema. *Sodas and candy are what people eat,* Tina thinks. *What is this stuff that these people are trying to make me eat?*

While that's hard to imagine, it reminds me of a conversation that I had with my longtime friend, Paige. Paige had been on a liquid protein diet and hadn't eaten a bite of food for several months. How she could cook wonderful meals every night for her husband and children amazed me. I asked her how she could do it. "Simple," she said. "Food no longer feels like it applies to me. I no more feel like people-food applies to me than I feel like our dog's food does. The sight and smell of people-food doesn't even tempt me any more than the sight and smell of our dog's food tempts me." That radical change in Paige's food schema helped me to understand how a foster child might not be tempted by a delicious meatloaf or steaming bowl of sweet peas and new potatoes.

Piaget also explained why people don't simply ignore new information instead of adding to or changing what's in their files. He called it *disequilibration.* Piaget explained that the normal drive of an organism is to *equilibrate* or balance itself. Imagine yourself walking along on the deck of a small boat. If the boat rocks to the right, you lean to the left. If it rocks to the left, you lean to the right. You are trying to re-balance or re-equilibrate yourself since you have found yourself unbalanced or disequilibrated. The theory suggests that when we are given new information that isn't in or doesn't fit with what is in our files, we are disequilibrated and have to deal with that new information in order to re-equilibrate ourselves. Thus, we accommodate by assimilating or accommodating our schema and we find ourselves re-equilibrated.

Having accommodated your schema about child development thus far, let's go on to explore the cognitive changes of children who are typically seven years old and entering concrete operations. Concrete operations is the stage of logical thought, which includes reversibility and decentration. However, these thinking skills are bound to concrete objects; they are not applicable to abstract thought.

Reversibility is the ability to mentally reverse events. While the preoperational child cannot backtrack in her thoughts in order to remember where she left her shoes, the concrete operational child can. Whereas the preoperational child may be able to tell you that $3 + 1 = 4$ but not be able to tell you that $4 - 1 = 3$, the concrete operational child can. Reversibility is why housemothers don't have to spend as much time helping ten-year-olds find lost shoes as they do three-year-olds. The ten-year-old can think backward or backtrack to where she left her shoes. The three-year-old can't. It works sort of like this.

The ten-year-old says to you, "Hey! I can't find my shoes!"

You say, "Think back and figure out where you last had them."

The ten-year-old thinks, "I just finished breakfast, and I don't have them. When I got up, they weren't by my bed. Where was I before bed? Oh, yeah. I watched TV last night. And I took them off and slid them under the couch." Off he goes to get his shoes.

The three-year-old says to you, "Where are my shoes?"

You say, "Think back and figure out where you last had them."

The three-year-old thinks, "My shoes are not here. Where are they?" The three-year-old simply does not have the ability to backtrack to where she left her shoes.

Decentration is the ability to focus on more than one aspect of a problem at a time. Unlike the preoperational child, who when told to clean up her room only picks up the toys and leaves the bed unmade because she has only focused on the floor, the concrete operational child is able to focus on all the types of mess in the bedroom. Exactly as you suspected, he doesn't clean up his room because he doesn't want to.

Please note that I am utterly convinced that my husband is an exception to the rule. I believe that when he steps over a wet towel that he left in the floor of the bedroom, he does so not because he is trying to aggravate me, but because he has not yet achieved perceptual decentration.

The concrete operational child has also reached the stage at which she understands that a long, skinny piece of cake may be as big as a short, fat piece. However, no living soul has ever figured out how to divvy up the fancy icing decorations. Is the big, purple rose on the corner of the cake worth eight of the fancy shell-things along the border or twelve of them? Or is the big, purple rose incomparable to any other object in existence? If anyone figures this out, would you please contact me? I find myself cowering in the corner at children's birthday parties when it gets close to the time to cut the cake.

A final aspect of concrete operations involves the notion of *multiple classifications*. For example, suppose you give a preoperational child some large and plastic circles, triangles, and squares and some are red, some blue, and some yellow. The preoperational child will classify them by one dimension: either color, shape, or size. The concrete operational child will classify them in a variety of ways employing all the dimensions. She may have large red circles, small red circles, large red triangles, and so on.

The lure of the act of classification is strong at this age. Concrete operational children love to classify and reclassify things. Rocks, Barbie clothes, and Secret Treasures stored away in shoeboxes are favorites for classification. But I'll bet you know what the biggie is. Baseball cards. Gazillions of dollars each year are made by gurus who understand the urge to classify that erupts in small boys who have reached the stage of concrete operations.

The thing that eleven- and twelve-year-old girls like to classify is boys, both those at school and those on TV and radio. When I was a twelve-year-old girl, we had slam books. For those of you who don't remember slam books, they were spiral notebooks in which the owner wrote a question on each page. Then each of her friends signed her name by a number in the back of the book, after which she went through the book and answered the question on each page by writing down her answer and her assigned number. These were essentially classification questions: What boys do you think are cute? What boys would you like to go on a date with? What boys do you like, but only as a friend? What boys would you let get to first base when you are sixteen? What boys would you let to get to second base when you are sixteen? And so on. The lure wasn't in thinking about boys so much as it was in classifying them. Only later did the lure become thinking about them.

Houseparents need to understand a youngster's biological imperative to classify for several reasons. First, it helps the houseparent to understand what may appear to be obsessive behavior as the child spends hours with her collections of odd and inconsequential items. Second, it helps the houseparent to understand much of the mess in children's rooms. To the houseparent, the Hot Wheels on the dresser are a mess to be reckoned with. But to the child, the cars are treasures to be classified and reclassified until the biological imperative to classify diminishes. I suppose that in hunter-gatherer societies, children gather and classify dead bugs. So unless you have a budding entomologist, be grateful that you are only grappling with baseball card, toy car, and doll clothes collectors.

Sometime around the age of eleven or twelve, developmentally normal children enter the stage of formal operations, the stage at which they gain the ability to think logically using abstract ideas. That is why teenagers drive us crazy. Suddenly they can think about things that are not tangible. Before, they either cleaned up their rooms simply because we said to, or else they didn't clean up their rooms because they didn't want to. Now, not only do they not clean up their rooms, but they subject us to reigns of terror by assaulting us with logical arguments. "If I make my bed now, I will only have to unmake it after I go to bed. So why should I make it at all? It's just a waste of time." I can't make a case against that. I can't figure out why beds ought to be made every day, so I end up making some dumb answer like, "Because I *said* so, that's why!"

I once read somewhere that when her child gave her the line about not making his bed because he would only have to unmake it later, a wise mother responded, "Then I'm not going to wash your dishes, because you're only going to put food on them again later." I don't remember whether Erma Bombeck said that or someone else did, but whoever she was, she could make a million bucks training the rest of us to out-logic our kids.

The nice thing about working with other people's kids who are at the stage of formal operations is that now, for the first time, you can reason with them. As a younger child, Tina could understand that Mommy is sick, but she couldn't understand why she can't live at home with Mommy, anyway. The formal operational child can understand the logical abstract argument about why she can't go home. Of course, that doesn't mean that she has to like it.

One of the less charming aspects of logical abstract thought is seen when the teenager says, "You're not my mother (or father)! I don't have to do what you say!" The younger child does what we say simply because in his mind, kids have to do things that grown-ups tell them to. The teenager can employ logic to determine that he doesn't have to do things simply because we tell him to. He realizes that we may be able to take away his privileges, restrict him to his room, or even paddle him. But we can't physically *force* him to make his bed if he resists. Of course, we can make his life unpleasant enough that he *wants* to make his bed simply to reduce the unpleasantness, but that doesn't mean that we can force him to make the bed if he sets his mind up not to.

If we are savvy, we will use logic to win the teenager over, rather than to try to coerce him. While he may resist our argument at the time at which we argue with him, given a little space and some cooling-off time, he will usually come around to our way of thinking. When we tell him, "I know that it's a pain to have to make your bed every day, and I know that I'm not your mom. But you live in our group home. So legally, I am acting as your mom. And while I understand that you don't want to make your bed, and I don't want to make mine either, we both have to. We are under certain rules and regulations by the state, and one of them is that we maintain a neat home. Why don't I help you make your bed, and then sometime when I need help, you can help me make mine?"

Piaget devised several reasoning problems to test whether a child was at the concrete operational or the formal operational stage. One type of test involves a problem similar to the following: Suppose that you are standing in front of a table. To the right of the table is a floor lamp. To the left of the table is a wing chair. Behind the table is a plant stand. Now imagine that you have moved so that the table is behind the floor lamp. From your new position, where is the chair? The plant stand?

The formal operational child will be able to reason through this problem, whereas the concrete operational child will not. If you are unable to reason through this problem, don't tell your direct supervisor. If your direct supervisor finds out, explain to her that Piaget explained that simply because we can operate at the abstract level in many areas, we can't necessarily operate at the abstract level in all areas. That should impress her.

In this chapter, we have discussed Piaget's notion of adaptation and of its sub-operations, assimilation and accommodation. We have talked about disequilibration and why we are driven to re-equilibrate ourselves. We have outlined concrete operational thought and abstract operational thought. In the next chapter, we will discuss the moral development of children.

Chapter 4

HOW KIDS THINK ABOUT RIGHT AND WRONG

In the last chapter, we completed our discussion of the intellectual development of children from Piaget's perspective. In this chapter, we will discuss the moral development of children. We will use two perspectives: that of Kohlberg and that of Gilligan. Kohlberg's perspective has historically been the old standard. Gilligan's is much newer. Kohlberg's perspective has been called a morality of justice, while Gilligan's has been called a morality of caring.

When Lawrence Kohlberg was a young doctoral student in psychology, he was assigned to complete an internship at a mental hospital. Kohlberg noted that the hospital was using electroshock not only as a therapeutic treatment but also to punish unruly patients. He wanted to take a stand against this terrible practice, so he started wearing badly mismatched socks. When he was criticized for wearing a red sock with a blue one, he told his superiors that this was his way of protesting the immoral use of electric shock.

Perhaps spurred on by the immoral behavior of the personnel at the mental hospital, Kohlberg went on to study moral development. Piaget had studied moral development, and he had used stories to assess a person's level of moral development. Kohlberg was heavily influenced by Piaget's work, so he, too, used stories. These stories were called *moral dilemmas.*

The most famous story that Kohlberg used is popularly known as Heinz's dilemma. Here it is:

> In Europe a woman was near death from cancer. One drug might save her, a form of radium a druggist in the same town had recently discovered. The druggist was charging $2,000, ten times what the drug cost him to make. The sick woman's husband, Heinz, went to everyone he knew to borrow the money, but he could only get together about half of what it cost. He told the druggist that his wife was dying and asked him to sell it cheaper, or let him pay later, but the druggist said no. The husband got desperate and broke into the man's store

to steal the drug for his wife. Should the husband have done that? Why? (Kohlberg, 1969, p. 367)

By classifying the way his interviewees answered the questions like Heinz's dilemma, Kohlberg identified six stages of moral reasoning. Kohlberg divided the six stages into three levels: *preconventional morality, conventional morality,* and *postconventional morality.*

Preconventional morality begins at birth and typically lasts until nine years of age. However, a number of children who end up in foster care never develop beyond the first stage of preconventional morality, which is the *Punishment-Obedience Level.* This stage is sometimes called the *Pleasure-Pain Level,* because the child at this stage does what feels good and doesn't do what brings pain. A person who if functioning at the Stage 1 of moral development might answer Heinz's dilemma by saying, "Heinz shouldn't have stolen the drug because he might get arrested."

One of my favorite examples of a child at Stage 1 morality concerns not one of my children when I was a houseparent, but one of my students. This little guy, Trevor, was a high school student who still functioned at Stage 1. One day, I had to answer a telephone call during regular class hours. (It happened to be my doctor, and you know how hard those people are to get in touch with.) My students knew that I had only two ironclad rules in class and one of them was: If for any reason I have to leave the room, no one may get out of their seat. The kids were great about this, and I had never had to deal with anyone breaking this rule.

Now, it's important to note that I did not have a condition set up to deal with people who would break this rule, because I knew that there was a wide range of moral development among my students. I taught high school resource room, so I had students who ranged in chronological age from 14 to 20, in mental age from 6 to 20, and in moral development from Level 1 to Level 4. Therefore, I knew that what would motivate one student toward moral behavior would not affect another student at all. So, Trevor *did* know not to get out of his seat, but he did *not* know what would happen if he violated this rule.

Now, I used a family metaphor to structure my classroom, so Trevor, one of the youngest boys, knew that he was supposed to stay in his seat and obey his older "brothers and sisters," but he didn't know what would happen if he didn't obey them. Besides, he figured that when I returned and they told me that he had been out of his seat, he would simply deny it and it would be his word against theirs. What he didn't think about was that since he situated himself where he could watch my return out the window, I, likewise, could see him standing up through the window.

When I entered the classroom, the older "sisters and brothers" said, "Trevor got up out of his seat, and when we told him that he knew the rule and to sit back down, he said that you'd never believe us! And that he was going to do whatever he wanted to!"

Of course, Trevor lied to me. After all, the Stage 1 child is motivated by seeking pleasure and avoiding pain, so why would he tell me the truth? I punished him by placing him in time out (a punishment which social teenagers devoutly despise), and knowing that violating my rule would bring him pain, he never got up when I had to leave the room after that.

Stage 2 moral development is called the *Instrumental Exchange Orientation.* Most people know it as "You scratch my back, I'll scratch yours." A typical answer to Heinz's dilemma by a child at Stage 2 is, "Heinz shouldn't steal from the druggist, and the druggist should be nice to Heinz." Among kids in my group home, "You don't tell on me and I won't tell on you," was an example of this stage.

A better example is this. When working with Dennis, a Stage 2 boy, I would say, "You help me clean the kitchen and then I'll help you with your laundry." This worked much better than saying, "You have to help me clean the kitchen and then you have to do your laundry." If Dennis didn't see any advantage to helping me clean the kitchen, he would be much less likely to comply without a major fight than if he saw my scratching his back in return.

In normal development, Conventional Morality begins at about nine years of age. Among most people, it continues throughout adulthood. The first stage of conventional morality, Stage 3, is called the *Interpersonal Conformity Orientation.* This stage is also called the *Good Boy/Nice Girl Stage.* The motivating force in this stage is approval of others. A typical response to Heinz's dilemma at this stage is, "If Heinz steals, other people won't like him."

Early in the stage, until about age twelve or thirteen, the approval sought is that of parents and teachers. After that, the approval sought is that of peers. This is why Renee was so helpful to you when she was ten or eleven years old, and then at twelve or thirteen shifted to being the Child from Hell who didn't give a rip about what you wanted.

Again, it's useful to look at my students instead of the children in my cottage, because I had the same students for four years at a time, and I only stayed with the children in my cottage for eighteen months.

Lora came to me when she was thirteen and stayed with me until she graduated at seventeen. Because she was a slow learner and that was reflected in her moral development, she was motivated by my approval from the time she became my student until well after her sixteenth birthday. Only then did the approval of her peers become more important than my approval.

This child would work hard for me and do everything I asked of her so that I would approve of her. But sometime during her sixteenth year, she began engaging in activities that she knew I would frown upon. For example, it was at that time that she began smoking, drinking, and having sex with her boyfriend. These behaviors earned her the approval of her peers. And especially of her boyfriend. Absolutely nothing I (or her parents) could do or say would change her behavior.

When I have had problems in the classroom with a late-stage Stage 3 child, I have called upon the other students to be my allies. Since I had close relationships with most of my students, I could call them aside individually or in a group and say, "Look guys, Sheila is really causing problems in the class. Your attention and approval is what she's after, and you know that my being kind and trying to talk to her about her behavior isn't working. What I have to ask of you is that you stop reinforcing her when she acts out like that. Ignore her, and when she looks at you and grins for you to applaud her misbehavior, turn away. Don't let her use you in this power struggle with me."

That generally worked for me. However, in this particular case, with Sheila, it didn't. Then I had to pull out the big guns. The biggest gun with teenagers is embarrassment.

Did you know that teenagers fear being embarrassed almost equally with the death of their parents? Since embarrassment is so powerful, it's a moral dilemma in itself as to when it's moral to use it to change behavior. Only three times in my many years of teaching, and never as a houseparent, did I ever resort to embarrassing a child.

The first case was Misty. Misty was actually a Stage 1 child, but at 14, one of the great pleasures she sought was attention from the boys in my class. And with her tattoos, her denim jacket, her raven hair against her ivory skin, and the five pierced earrings in each ear, she got the attention of the boys. One of the many ways that she chose to get their attention was to squeal and giggle whenever I or anyone else said anything that she might twist around to be a sexual innuendo. This created untold problems in my literature/social studies class in which I used novels to teach the students about psychology and sociology and how those things related to their real lives. It was essential that I create an attitude of seriousness and compassion in this class so that students would feel free to talk about issues that worried them in their own lives as we followed the lives of the characters in the books.

After working with Misty for almost two years, I had tried everything I knew of short of embarrassing her. Placing her in time out hadn't worked, because she would just write letters to boys while she sat there. If I didn't let her have any paper, she would take a nap. If I assigned her to detention hall, she would simply amass the detentions and never serve them. If she were suspended for failing to serve her detentions, she would consider it a holiday, which, since her mother didn't support the school, it was. Since she was legally diagnosed as a child with a behavior disorder, we couldn't expel her. So she was all mine.

Finally, I decided that I would have to resort to embarrassing Misty. Because I knew that this breach of my normal behavior would upset the rest of my students, I carefully prepared them for it. On Friday, one of the many days that Misty didn't come to school, I said, "Look guys, you know how Misty has been tearing up our classroom. Right?"

The students agreed.

"I've tried being kind and loving and understanding of her behavior, right?"

The students agreed. "I don't know how or why you act so nice to her," Mary said, and Shannon agreed. Even the boys nodded their heads.

"Well, she has problems," I said, "and I wanted to try to love her through them, but it hasn't worked."

The kids agreed that it sure as the devil hadn't.

"Then I tried talking to her about the way she acts, placing her in time out, giving her detention, but none of that worked."

"You oughta whip her," one student said.

"Well," I answered, "First of all, I don't believe in hitting people, and second of all, we don't paddle people here at the high school."

"So what are you going to do?" asked Mary. "She ruins our sessions because whenever anyone is trying to talk about their problems, she starts laughing, like they were talking about sex when they weren't."

Joyce nodded her head. "Yeah, like when I said, 'I can't remember that guy's name . . . It's right on the tip of my tongue,' and she acted like I was doing sex with him because I said tongue."

"Or like when I said I wanted to get together with my cousin this weekend, and she acted like I meant I wanted to have sex with her," said Heather.

"What *are* you going to do?" asked Dave. "It was funny at first, but now it's just sick."

"What I'm going to do is nail her to the wall," I said. "The next time that she ruins our session, I'm going to let my natural anger work for me. Instead of bridling it and being gentle with her, I'm going to let her rip. I'm going to yell, and scream, and get right up in her face. But it's important that you understand this. I am not out of control. Let me repeat that. *I am not out of control.* I will yell at her. I will get in her face not because I am out of control but because I have tried everything else I know to do and this is my last resort. And since I am her last shot at staying in the public school in this town, I have to try this. I have talked to her counsellor and he has agreed that I have to do something different, so this is my last stand. My behavior will be based upon a clinical decision and not because I have lost my self-control.

"So don't be afraid. I'm not angry with any of you. Don't think I am. In fact, I need your help. I need you to sit quietly while I have a chew on her, and then go right back to the story with me and ignore whatever response she makes. Because she may well come back with some tacky reply to try and win your approval. So don't let her, okay?"

The kids nodded. "It's about time you did something about her," said Aaron.

I didn't have to wait long to try Operation Chew Her Out. The following Monday, when we were reading the story about a girl whose sister was dying, we came to a passage where she described the coming of spring. When Heather, who was reading aloud for us, read the word *pussywillows,* Misty snorted and gave a raucous laugh. Then she turned to the boys sitting at her right and left around our table and grinned. One of the boys looked up at me expectantly and that's when I let loose.

I leaned across the table and told her how sick and tired I was of her foul mouth and making sexual innuendos out of nonsexual things and that I wasn't going to take it any more. I ranted and raved for what must have been the better part of five minutes. With my eyes narrowed to slits, I hissed a warning to her to never make the mistake of taking my gentleness for weakness. "My gentleness is borne out of my strength, not out of weakness. And don't you ever forget it!" I seethed.

No one else in the room so much as moved a muscle. Misty stared at me, wide-eyed. She didn't make a sound for the rest of the hour. She hung around quietly for a few more days, then quit coming to school altogether.

By resorting to embarrassment, I solved the problem of my class being disrupted. But I also created the situation which I am sure resulted in her quitting school. So, was it a moral thing for me to have done? I really don't know. I don't think it was a moral thing to do. Misty's quitting school was not what I wanted. I wanted her to turn herself around and start trying to win approval for doing positive things instead of negative ones. Remember this story if you are ever driven to considering using embarrassment to change the behavior of a late Stage 3 child.

Stage 4 is the second half of the Conventional Level. Stage 4 is called the *Law-and-Order Orientation.* Many people think that this stage is a bad one, because the term *law'n'order* has come to be associated with poorly educated, red-neck, narrow-minded people. But that wasn't what Kohlberg had in mind at all. He was referring to people who act in a given way because they believe that the laws established by a society are established for the good of all. They recognize that the combined wisdom of the group is usually superior to their own wisdom at any one time. Therefore, the Stage 4 person would say something like this to Heinz's dilemma: "It is against the law to steal. If we all broke the law whenever we wanted to, then society would crumble."

My favorite Stage 4 story concerns a couple of children I heard about who weren't at Stage 4 at all, but the story makes a point. The children were two first graders who were in the bathroom off of the classroom when the fire bell rang. The teacher hurried the class out of the room forgetting the two children who were in the lavatory. When the little ones came out of the bathroom and into the classroom, everyone was gone and the fire bell was still ringing. But the children knew the rule that no one was allowed to get out of their seats without permission. So they sat in their seats and cried, believing that they were going to die in a fire.

The problem with Stage 4 thinking is that even when laws are wrong or immoral, Stage 4'ers believe that those laws should be obeyed anyway. For example, Stage 4'ers believe that if the law says that Jews must be sent to the gas chamber, then so be it. After all, the law is the law. (Thank God for people who lay down their lives to change immoral laws.)

This brings us to Stage 5: the *Prior Rights and Social Contract Orientation*. People at this stage believe that laws must be evaluated. If they are laws which are based on the social contract (the mutual agreement between a rational, moral individual and society that these laws protect that individual's rights), then the laws should be obeyed. But if the laws are not based upon the social contract, then those laws must not be obeyed and must be changed. The civil rights movement of the 1960s was conducted because of people who were operating at Stage 5.

A person at Stage 5 might answer Heinz's dilemma thus: "Sometimes you have to break the law. One of those times might be when breaking the law saves someone's life."

Stage 6 is the *Universal Ethical Principles Orientation*. At this stage, justice is based upon self-chosen, but not self-serving, principles. Stage 6'ers would obey laws because they generally are founded upon such principles. But when a law violates one of these principles, then that law is disobeyed, even to the point of death. Stage 6 morality is based on the abstractions of comprehensiveness, universality, consistency, and reciprocity, as is the golden rule. This is contrasted with the concreteness of the Ten Commandments. Either you steal or you don't by the latter. By the former, you choose which to do based upon the entire situation. Therefore, a Stage 6 person might answer Heinz's dilemma by saying, "The decision on whether or not to steal must consider all the factors involved. Sometimes, stealing is the morally right thing to do."

Now that you know what Stage 6 is, I have to tell you that Kohlberg says that he has never been able to find anyone who was developed to that level. However, he argues that the stage exists, at least in theory.

Although I told you that Kohlberg developed a six-stage theory, in 1985 he wrote a book in which he said that he had added a seventh stage. He said that the people that reached this stage were very old people who had developed a spiritual understanding of the interconnectedness of all life. Kohlberg said that these folks had three options from which to select their spirituality. They might believe in God as in the Hebrew, Christian, or Islamic tradition. They might be pantheistic (believe in the presence of God in all things). Or they might be agnostic cosmologists (not believe that there is enough evidence to either prove God exists or doesn't exist, but believe that each person is part of the great connectedness of all that is). But whatever spiritual option they choose, Kohlberg said that a number of very old people reach this seventh stage.

Now that we've discussed Kohlberg's perspective on moral development, let us turn to Gilligan's perspective of moral development, the Morality of Caring.

Carol Gilligan studied Kohlberg's work and felt like something important was missing. Kohlberg's theory had been developed exclusively on a longitudinal (over a long time) study of males; females had not been included in the studies upon which Kohlberg's theory of morality was based. As a result, when other studies that classified males and females according to their moral stages were conducted, a disproportionate number of females were placed in Stage 3 as compared to Stage 4. "Something's going on here," thought Gilligan. She suggested that more women fell into Stage 3 because women are more compassionate and empathetic to other people and are more sensitive to relationships than men are. Therefore, women continued to care about what other people thought (and felt) more than they cared about law and order. Based upon this notion and her studies of real-life dilemmas experienced by the women whom she interviewed, Gilligan developed a model of moral development. In contrast to Kohlberg's morality of justice, Gilligan's model describes a morality of *care and responsibility.*

Gilligan's first level is called *Individual Survival.* Like Kohlberg's Punishment-Obedience Level, the individual at this stage serves her own purpose; however, unlike Kohlberg, the emphasis is on doing what you have to do to survive rather than on feeding greedy, self-serving desires. For example, from Kohlberg's perspective, Donita would steal food from the cottage refrigerator because she's a selfish little heathen who is greedy and figures she can get away with it. From Gilligan's perspective, Donita steals food because she's gone without food before, and she's trying to assure her survival by creating a stockpile. (Would all of you who have never had a child in your care steal food please stand up?)

Next comes a transition level from Stage 1 to Stage 2 that Gilligan calls Stage 1A. Stage 1A is called *From Selfishness to Responsibility.* During this transition stage, Donita begins to realize that caring for others rather than just caring for oneself is the moral thing to do.

Stage 2 in Gilligan's model is the stage of *Self-Sacrifice and Social Conformity.* This level is similar to Kohlberg's Stage 3. From Kohlberg's perspective then, Donita behaves in a certain way in order that chosen people will consider her "good." However, Gilligan argues that it is important to understand that Donita behaves not for social approval but rather in order to care for others and to promote the welfare of the group. This stage has been identified as representing the conventional view of women as caretakers, nurtures, and protectors. At this stage, Donita would steal food because she didn't want her little sister, Consuela, to go hungry. From this perspective, stealing is the caring, loving, nurturing thing to do. Or Donita might not steal food, even if she was hungry, because she believed it was in the best interest of everyone in the cottage that she not steal food.

This is the stage at which many women remain. These women are identifiable by their martyrdom to their families. Some women wear this martyrdom gracefully; you never realize that they are self-sacrificing, because they do it so quietly. They go about their lives caring for others without drawing attention to their deeds. Other women, however, wear their self-sacrifice like a badge of honor. A neighbor told me of such an older woman at her church.

> I feel real sorry for Esther, but I don't like to be around her.... It's just that...well...you can't help someone who won't help themselves.... (Shrugs.) See, she's got these two grown daughters.... One of 'em's single and the other's got three little kids and (the daughters) both take advantage of her. She's always giving them money and taking care of the grandkids, but both of (the daughters) won't give her the time of day.... They just use her and she's always crying on my shoulder saying stuff like, "I've given my life for (the daughters) and all they do is use me!" I've told her to quit doing for 'em, but she says that without her, the single one won't have enough money, and the one with the kids wouldn't be able to keep her job without someone to take care of the kids.

This woman wears her martyrdom like a badge of honor, and alienates everyone around her.

The next stage is another transition stage called *From Goodness to Truth*. This stage, Stage 2A, is marked by a growing realization that in order to care for others, one must also take care of oneself. When a housemother refuses to answer the door on her day off, she may be refusing because she is self-centered; however, she may be refusing because she knows that unless she protects herself and takes care of herself by guarding her day off, she won't be able to nurture her kids well. It's important to understand that the motive for caring for oneself at this stage is very different than the motive for caring for oneself at Stage 1. Now, Donita may steal food for herself as well as Consuela, because she realizes that unless she stays healthy, there is no one to care for Consuela.

I think that may be part of the high burnout rate among houseparents; the parents are locked into Gilligan's Stage 2 morality, in which they have not yet come to the realization that they must take care of themselves if they are to continue to be able to care for the children in their home. On the other hand, maybe the high rate of burnout is due to the fact that the houseparents are in Stage 2A and have come to the realization that in order to take care of themselves so that they can continue to care for each other and their biological children, they must finally leave the emotionally draining atmosphere that child care can create.

While talking about moving from the level of caring for others at risk of detriment to one's well-being, I want to share a story about Mother Teresa of Calcutta. When Mother Teresa first began her mission in Calcutta, she would eat nothing but thin gruel like the desperately poor people she served. She went along in this way until she required the nuns serving under her supervision to eat the same substandard diet. At this point, the Roman Catholic church intervened and said that the nuns had to eat nutritious meals. As I recall, Mother Teresa resisted for a while but finally gave in.

That story gives me hope. Whereas I had always thought that Mother Teresa was born with a level of morality that I could never hope to achieve, seeing her operate at a lower level from the Gilliganian perspective and then growing into a higher level offers me a little hope. On the other hand, from a Kohlbergian perspective, maybe she was operating at Level 6 or 7 and did not eat because she believed it was unjust for some to eat while so many starved. If that's the case, then I never will be able to reach her level of moral development, because I'm just not made that way. Either way, I don't reckon that I'll ever get to ask her whether her reasoning was based on an ethic of justice or one of caring.

Gilligan's Stage 3 is called the *Morality of Nonviolence.* This stage is characterized by the ethic of the equality of self and others. This suggests that it is wrong to serve oneself at the expense of others. Lest we think about violence as being limited to physical violence, we should think again. When we gossip about another houseparent, we are committing an act of violence against her. We are serving ourselves at her expense. When we say something mean or unkind to a child in our home, we are committing an act of violence against him. We are serving ourselves at his expense. We feel better for having vented our feelings, but he has suffered a wound that he will remember always. (Note: Someone told me the other day that a research study found that you have to say thirteen positive things to a child to overcome the damage to self-esteem caused by saying one negative thing. Think about it.)

Some people have called Gilligan's model a feminist model of moral development. We do certainly think of women as being more nurturing than are men. However, in studies of both men and women in which decisions about moral development were based either upon justice or upon caring, researchers found that moral orientations are not predicated upon gender. That is, some women are motivated by caring while others are motivated by justice; some men are motivated by justice, while others are motivated by caring.

One thing that we need to consider is the effect of ethnic group on moral thinking. Kohlberg's work was conducted on white males. White American males are the most individualistic cultural group in the world. (They are followed closely by Australian, Canadian, and British males.) In contrast, African Americans, Hispanics, Native Americans, and Asians tend to be collectivistic. (Guatemalans are the most collectivistic cultural group in the world.) Collectivistic means that individuals place the welfare of the group ahead of their own personal desires. Since these groups value the good of the group over individual welfare, it may be that men in these groups are motivated by caring and responsibility rather than by justice.

If I have made you think that the levels of moral development are set in stone, let me assure you that they are not. They are more like Jello. We tend to be at one level, but under certain circumstances we operate at another level. For example, teenagers who are operating at Kohlberg's Law and Order Stage on abstract issues like Heinz's dilemma tend to operate one stage lower on issues which actually affect their everyday lives. One study asked teenagers whether it was morally wrong for them to engage in various degrees of premarital sexual activity at home when their parents were away. The teens overwhelmingly gave answers that reflected Level 3: they approved of whatever level of sexual activity that they believed their peers would approve of. Needless to say, quite a few of those kids said that it was morally right to engage in intercourse under the circumstances.

In this chapter, we have examined two models of moral development: Kohlberg's model of a morality of justice, and Gilligan's model of a morality of caring of responsibility. Now that you have a basic understanding of moral development, in the next chapter, we will explain to you how you can work to create a moral community within your cottage, residence hall, or home.

Chapter 5

CREATING A MORAL CLIMATE

In the last chapter, we discussed two models of moral development. In this chapter, I want to tell you about developing a climate in your cottage that promotes moral growth.

Thomas Likona developed a model of moral education which was designed to be used in public schools; however, you will quickly see how his model can apply to a group home. Likona's model suggests that four processes must operate in a group home if houseparents are to help children grow into moral adults. The first process is that the houseparents must *build children's self-esteem and their sense of social community.* The second is that houseparents must *encourage cooperative work and helping relations.* Third, houseparents must *get children to reflect upon moral issues.* Fourth, houseparents must *give children the opportunity to participate in decisions that affect their lives.* We'll discuss each of these processes in turn.

One facet of building self-esteem involves giving a child a sense of competence and mastery. When I first became a housemother, my supervisor, an MSW, told me, "A boy must feel that he knows every nick and cranny in his new environment. He needs time to explore the entire ranch. He needs to know what's under the cabinet in the kitchen, what's the third garment in the fourth stack of (new) clothes in the supply room, and what's stored in the dusty old box on the top shelf in the tack room of the barn. His first step toward self-esteem is feeling like he is the master of his environment."

You've seen children go through the drawer of your desk without your permission, haven't you? So have I. Especially during my years of teaching children with behavior problems, the first thing that I allowed many children to do was to go through my desk. Then they knew what was there and it was demystified for them. It also sent a big message: *You are welcome here. I am willing to share what I have with you.* Needless to say, things that I was not willing to share were not stored in my desk, but rather locked away in my file cabinet.

While I am not suggesting that you place things that you care about deeply in a personal area and then let the children have access to it, I am suggesting that you have some things that are not important to you stored in one of "your" areas that you are willing to give the children access to. Your ruler, pens, tape, and so forth are highly expendable and, if placed in your desk, make a child feel important when he knows that he can use your things if he needs to. I remember that my junior high band director, Mr. Wilson, would let us get pencils and such out of his desk drawer when we needed them. It made us feel important and special that we could have access to his personal pencils. Big deal? It is to a young person.

Another self-esteem builder is learning something special about each child and then making references to it. For example, William was an abused twelve-year-old who came to our cottage. He had a pure, clear soprano voice. When I learned that he could sing, I made frequent reference to his gift. Sometimes we would steal away together to the chapel and I would make bold but pitiful attempts at playing the piano while he sang. By making his singing something that was important to me, I was able to make William know that he was important to me. If you value a child and let him know it, then he will value himself more.

Of course, that doesn't apply just to children. As a forty-plus-year-old professor, when the director of my division at the university pats me on the back and tells me that he's happy with my work, it raises my self-esteem. Affirmation is a powerful force.

What I call affirmation is similar to what Robert Bly calls admiring. Bly, whose video with Bill Moyers, *A Gathering of Men,* and whose book, *Iron John,* were important milestones in the men's movement, said, "If you are an older man, and you are not admiring a young man, then you are harming him." By admiring a young man, Bly means affirming him. Praising him for his strengths. Telling him how proud you are of him because of what he is doing.

I don't know of anyone who has specifically said, "If you are an older woman, and you are not admiring a young woman, then you are harming her." Since I don't know of anyone who has said that, I will say it here. This is not to mean that I don't think women should not affirm boys or that men should not affirm girls. This is to mean that I want to make a point to encourage us older folks to affirm (admire) younger folks, regardless of their gender.

Virginia Klapperich was my mentor when I was a college student. Miss K, as we called her, has passed over to the other side, but the impact that she had on my life remains. Miss K admired me. She told me that I was bright and capable and a hard worker. She told me that I was going to make a difference in the lives of children who have disabilities. How could I not have had good self-esteem about my professional abilities?

In the same way, as a writer, when my editor dashes off a note to me telling me that my manuscript is "splendid," I walk around all day saying, "I write splendidly. I am a splendid writer." Then I go dash off another chapter. So affirmation or admiration is important to us at every stage of life.

In the same way that affirmation is so powerful, disaffirming statements wield as much power. I didn't realize how much power an older person's disaffirmation held over a younger person until I became a college professor. During my first semester as a professor, I received two papers from a faceless student that were very poorly written. Upon receiving the second of these papers, I jotted a note on the last page. I wrote, "Your writing needs a lot of work. Being an effective written communicator is an important part of being a teacher. You aren't ready to be admitted to the Division of Teacher Education until you do some remedial work on your writing. I would like to see you enroll in a writing course."

I promptly forgot about it. Two weeks later, when the next paper was handed in, a thirty-fiveish student hesitantly approached me. "Dr. Camerer," she said, "I'm the student that you wrote the note to about my writing. I hope you like this paper better. I really did my best. I cried and cried when you told me that I couldn't write. I hope you like this one okay." The very notion that I could make a student cry because I criticized her paper floored me. I have had similar incidents happen since then in a variety of ways. It took my adult students to teach me what I had never learned from my child students: that even mild criticism can crush the fragile flower of an ego.

This is not to say that you can't help children build strong self-esteem, unless you never correct them. This is to say that we gently, delicately, tenderly prune the flower bush. We don't jerk the whole thing out of the ground in our eagerness to improve it.

Another thing that a houseparent can do is to write notes to children. Finding an admiring note waiting for you on your bed when you get home from school is a heady experience. I'm not just talking about a note saying, "I love you," although that's great to hear, too. I'm talking about a note that praises and admires a specific thing that the child has done. "You made me feel so good inside when you earned that B on your science project! You are a hard worker and really smart, and I am so proud of you!" Let me note that this kind of message can be particularly powerful if it comes from a housedad. It often seems easier for women to offer affirmation than for men to, so a note from a housedad would be a treasure that a child would keep tucked away in his treasure box forever.

The second part of the process involved in building self-esteem and social community is building the social community. One important way that social community is built is through public sharing of personal feelings. You might have weekly group sharing sessions. During the years that I taught high school children with behavior and learning problems, we started every Monday morning with a group session. Starting with me, each one of us opened up and told the best thing, the worst thing, and the funniest thing about our week. This activity helped to knit us *closely* together. While the best and funniest things were important to share, the most important facet was sharing the worst thing. This expression of personal hurt or frustration helped us see that underneath the skin, we are all alike in our humanity, that we all bleed, and we all cry.

I want to stress the importance of my sharing my worst thing with the children. That may have been the catalyst in making these sessions affective in building community. I urge you to try right away to share a personal hurt with one of your kids and see if it doesn't help build an invisible bond between you.

Another interesting thing that builds community is eating together. Did you know that the word *family* is sometimes said to mean *those who eat together?* Think about it. *Famine* means being *without food.* Family means those who share food together. This brings up an important principle for houseparents: Food is never just something to eat. What that means is that food carries profound emotional messages. If I love you, I feed you. If I love you enough and you are young enough, I feed you from my own body. However, if I deny you food, I am telling you that you are not even worthy of human sustenance. Not even worthy of living. Think about that the next time you are tempted to send a child to bed without dessert.

This notion of eating together is a powerful community builder. But it can be even more powerful when it is conducted away from the usual home site. For example, one scientist examined ways of making co-workers develop closer bonds. The conclusions were these: if you want to build a strongly bonded team, have people eat and drink together, in a location away from the work site, talk about anything except work, and have no time limits. So how does that translate to houseparents building community? Perhaps where you live it means a trip to the beach for a cookout. Maybe it means a trip to a pizza restaurant. Or maybe it means hotdogs and sodas at the park. In any event, it means don't try to have dinner at home every night. Use some of your food allowance for community building outside of the cottage.

The last thing I want to say about community building before we move on comes from my own research. I studied teenagers who had satisfying friendships and those who did not. I wanted to know if their beliefs about friendship differed. I found out that they most assuredly did. The kids who had friends believed in sticking up for their friends. The kids who didn't have friends did not believe in sticking up for their friends. Now, I'm not saying that there may not be a number of other reasons that teenagers don't have satisfying friendships. I am simply saying that teenagers who don't stick up for their friends won't have satisfying friendships. And the notion of sticking up for friends included covering for your friends when they commit a wrongdoing. So don't be too hard on Evan when he covers up for Brandon who was smoking in the bathroom. And don't be too hard on Tomas when he stands up to you to defend Tony. What they are doing is building community. And without community, you will never create a psychological climate which promotes moral development.

According to Dr. Lickona, the next process required in order to create an atmosphere which promotes moral development is having children work in cooperative groups. Instead of assigning one child to dust the living room and another child to pick up the room, have the children work together to accomplish each task. It may be hard to get the children to start working together. Kids who have always seen other kids as competitors will probably have a hard time learning to see other kids as helpmates and partners. These kids may intentionally subvert your attempt to get them to work cooperatively together. Don't give up. Keep monitoring and encouraging the work teams.

Having a group reward for teams who do their chores well together can often be a highly motivating force for them to learn to work together. A reward that can only be earned by the two working together, as opposed to one child working alone, can work wonders. One way that you can do this is to set a very short time limit on the chores, one that no one person could possibly meet alone.

A word of warning: don't start out two kids who hate each other as partners when you change chores from individual chores to group chores. It will never work. It's easier if you start out partnering kids who have some natural affinity for each other. Of course, some kids don't like anyone, and no one likes them. That presents a challenge when teaching kids cooperative work arrangements and helping relations.

One activity that may work in your cottage to improve your children's attitudes toward helping each other is having an evening appreciation time. This constitutes having each person in the cottage tell what she appreciated that day that another person did. Giving this special attention to appreciated behaviors reinforces those behaviors. I have used this activity in the past; however, one problem is that some children never think to be helpful to others, so are never singled out and appreciated before the group. They may require some direct instruction from you to help another resident.

The third process in Dr. Lickona's model of moral education is moral reflection. Moral reflection refers to thinking about moral issues. These issues can be real ones that occur in the cottage. They can also be issues encountered in novels, and there are a ton of great children's and adolescents' novels on the market that deal with every issue under the sun.

When an issue arises in the cottage or in a novel that you are reading with the group during the evening, the children should be challenged to think about, discuss, and perhaps debate the issue. You need to be present to provide input to the kids when they are discussing moral behaviors; this really isn't something that you want to leave them alone to do. Many children in basic care have had very poor adult role models for moral behavior.

Kohlberg uses a "plus-one" technique in leading discussions of moral behavior. If Jared were operating on Level 2 of Kohlberg's model, then Kohlberg would ask him a question that would push him toward beginning to develop Level 3 thinking. For example, suppose you are discussing boys taking each other's belongings without permission. Jared says, "You shouldn't do that because if you take someone else's stuff, then they will take yours."

You respond with a Level 3 type of answer, "What do you think other people think about someone who takes other people's belongings?"

You are gently presenting Jared with moral reasoning from the next stage. He may be far from internalizing that kind of moral thought, but you will keep presenting him with fuel for his moral fire.

Lest you think, "Oh, yeah, right. I can really see these hooligans of mine sitting around reading a book and talking about moral issues," think again. The most successful program I had in working with teenagers who had behavior problems was just that: reading captivating adolescent novels and discussing the moral conflicts that arose. You won't believe it until you try it. I won't try to name books here that would make wonderful moral discussion fodder for you, but your local children's librarian can help you.

Lickona says that the fourth process is participatory decision making. This holds children accountable for decisions that affect the quality of the cottage life. Problems in the cottage are not treated as isolated issues in which one person is singled out. Instead, problems are considered by the cottage as a whole. If one problem in the cottage is that too many people are trying to use the washing machine on Sunday night, then the children can approach this as a problem that they need to consider together and solve. The resulting sense of group responsibility helps children feel like colleagues in ownership of the cottage. In this way, children participate in establishing cottage rules.

A warning: the four processes involved in Lickona's moral education program do not work in isolation from each other. If you want one pineapple, you have to buy the whole bushel. This isn't a program where you take what appeals to you and ignore the rest; you won't develop an atmosphere conducive to moral development. It may be more demanding of you than just saying, "You broke a rule. You're on detention," but it will be worth it. Putting this program in place demands houseparents who care deeply about the importance of moral education and are committed to investing the emotional energy to wade through what will be difficult beginnings.

In this chapter, we have looked at an excellent way of developing a climate conducive to moral development in your cottage. In the next chapter, we will examine the psychosocial development of children and adults.

Chapter 6

HOW KIDS DEVELOP PSYCHOSOCIALLY

In the last chapter we discussed ways that a caretaker who is raising other people's kids can create an environment in the home or on the floor that will promote moral growth. In this chapter, we will discuss how children and adults develop in the psychosocial realm.

We can't think about psychosocial development without talking about Erik Erikson. No, that's not the name of some new rock group, like Erik Erikson and the Screaming Norsemen. Erik Erikson is the man whose name is most often associated with psychosocial development and who gave us the idea of identity crisis.

Erik Homberg Eriksen was born in Frankfurt, Germany in 1902, and he only died a couple of years before the publication of this book. Right up to the end of his life, he and his co-researcher/wife continued thinking about the notion of psychosocial development. It was his thinking about psychosocial development of very old people while he, himself, was over ninety that led him to some insights about great age that no one else had shared with the scientific community.

Eriksen's father abandoned his mother around the time Erik was born. His mother married a local physician who raised Erik as his own, and helped his mother keep from Erik the secret that his biological father had abandoned him. This created a rather odd problem for Erik. Because both his mother and his adoptive father were Jewish, but Erik looked strikingly Danish (tall, blonde, and blue-eyed), he was rejected by the other kids at school. The Jewish children called him "the goy" (non-Jew), while the Gentiles called him "the Jew." He felt like he didn't fit in anywhere. It's not surprising, then, that he not only did rather poorly in school but that he dropped out before graduating.

(That's something important to think about. When harassment by peers contributes to a man like Erik Eriksen dropping out of school, son of a doctor who had all the advantages, then its no wonder that many of our children drop out of school when other kids make fun of them for being "boys' ranchers" or the like. And since much of the rejection was

45

caused by his looking different from his supposed cultural group, it's no wonder that it's so important for our kids to have clothes that fit in with the majority of kids at school.)

After dropping out of high school, Eriksen skipped college and began wandering about Europe. He was an artist, and he was looking for a sense of purpose and meaning for his art. He finally tired of wandering and took a job at an American school in Vienna, Austria. While he was there, he met Anna Freud, daughter of the famed Sigmund Freud. Under Anna's influence, Erik began to study Freud's psychoanalytic theory and began psychoanalysis under her. The psychoanalysis helped him understand his unhappy childhood and the restlessness that had dominated his youth. Eriksen was so impressed by how psychoanalysis had helped him that he began studying under Sigmund Freud at the Vienna Psychoanalytic Institute and graduated in 1933. Pretty good for a high school dropout.

Since 1933 was the year that Hitler came into power in Germany, Eriksen moved to America. He became Boston's first child analyst. He then enrolled in graduate school at Harvard, but never finished. In 1939, the year that the Nazis invaded Poland, Eriksen became a U.S. citizen.

Over the next several years, Eriksen taught at Yale and on a reservation in South Dakota. He finally landed at the University of California where he was fired in an incident that must have had a profound effect on his thinking. The incident took place during the McCarthy era.

All faculty of the University of California were required to sign a loyalty oath. Having seen what blind obedience to your country could do in Nazi Germany, Eriksen refused to sign. He was fired, then reinstated because the powers that be decided that even though he hadn't signed the statement, he wasn't going to blow up any buildings or leak secrets about students' grades to the Communists. However, he resigned the reappointment, because other faculty who had refused to sign had not also been reinstated.

Eriksen then returned to Massachusetts and set up a clinical practice where he began to write over the next twenty years. In 1960, he took a professorship at Harvard and remained with them until he retired from the university. However, he never retired from thinking about and refining his work.

With the influence of his life in mind, let's begin to look at Eriksen's theory of psychosocial development.

Like Piaget, Eriksen believed that development took place in stages.

He also believed that there are critical periods in development. He called these critical periods *crises*. Compare this to the development of an unborn fetus. As childcare providers, we have all worked with children who have brain damage caused by a mother who drank or used other drugs while she was pregnant. What you may not know is that in addition to the damage caused by a mother who drinks throughout her pregnancy, a mother can damage her fetus by having only one or two drinks during her pregnancy, if the drinks are taken during a critical moment of the baby's development. Thinking about this will help you better understand Eriksen's crises in psychosocial development.

The first stage is the crisis of *Trust vs. Mistrust.* This stage begins the moment of birth and continues to from one to one and a half years. It is at this stage that an infant either learns that his mother can be counted on to take care of him, or he learns that she can't be counted on. Based upon this, he either develops basic trust or he develops basic mistrust of people. After all, if you can't depend on your own mom, who can you depend on? (Of course, when I say "Mom" you know that I am referring to the baby's primary caregiver, whomever that may be.)

Eriksen explained that trust is developed as a result of "consistency, continuity, and sameness of experience." If the baby's needs are met with this consistency, continuity, and sameness of experience, then the baby learns trust. *Yesterday I cried and Mom fed me,* thinks Baby. *Today if I cry, she will feed me again. That's the way things work. I can count on Mom to take care of me.*

Feeding, in fact, is the important event in the development of basic trust. But what about if the baby's basic physiological needs are met (he is fed, etc.) but without warmth and caring? In other words, the baby is handed his bottle, but he is not snuggled and cuddled and cooed? At best, he will develop mistrust, and at worst, he will actually die. Believe it or not, a loving, caring, nurturing attitude in a mother is essential. That is why so many babies die in orphanages in places like Romania; they are fed and clothed, but they're not cuddled and loved.

Keeping in mind the trust vs. mistrust crisis, why do you think so many of our children in basic care come to us with such severe problems? Many of our kids have been abused. They have learned that people can't be trusted. Most of our kids have been neglected. They have learned that people can't be trusted. It's no wonder that it's so difficult to parent other people's kids. The one thing that many of the kids learned from their own parents is that people can't be trusted.

It is important to note that even a good mother, if she has to be separated from her baby at this stage (if, for example, she is injured in a serious accident and hospitalized for a period of time), inadvertently teaches her baby that people can't be trusted. I can't overstate enough the importance of the uninterrupted mother-child bond at this stage of life.

Before we leave Stage 1, it is important to add one last thing. Eriksen said that healthy development is a balance between trust and mistrust that results from a parental relationship which is neither too indulgent nor too harsh. While we definitely want to produce individuals who have a good sense of trust, we don't want to produce gullible individuals. Eriksen argued that gullibility is the result of overindulging a baby at Stage 1. From this perspective, we can think of the crisis as a continuum. We want the baby to develop well on the trust side of the center of the continuum, but we do want him to be mistrustful of the guy who tries to sell him the Brooklyn Bridge or a piece of waterfront property in Arizona.

The second stage is *Autonomy vs. Shame and Doubt.* This stage runs from about a year and a half to three years. Autonomy refers to a sense of independence. The important event at this stage is toilet training, although walking, grasping, dressing, and such are also important tasks in the development of autonomy.

The toddler needs to explore her environment in order to gain a sense of independence. Do you remember my supervisor who said that our boys' ranchers needed to explore every nook and cranny in order to feel masters of their environment? This is where that need starts. If Becky tries to take an interesting-looking object off the shelf and Dad stops her, then that contributes to the development of shame and doubt. I'm not saying that you have to let Becky have your precious fly-tieing set; what I am saying is that if you don't want Becky to explore something, then it should be stored safely out of her way. Things that are stored within her three-foot world need to be things that she can investigate.

In the same way, if Becky makes a mess while she is trying to feed herself, let her make the mess. Don't take over and feed her yourself because it's neater and faster. She needs to develop the sense of being able to do things for herself.

It is the drive to autonomy that creates the Terrible Twos. The word "NO!" is direct evidence that a child has entered this stage. Dad wants Becky to put on her shoes. Becky says, "NO!" Mom wants Becky to eat her muffin. Becky says, "NO!" Becky is showing the world that she can now make decisions for herself. Sometimes she is going to make messes for herself, but unless they are potentially serious messes (such as sticking her tongue into an electrical outlet), let her make them. If the mess is no more serious than that she dresses herself with one sock inside out, let her dress herself with one sock inside out. Children who are never allowed to make messes and gain a feeling of control of their lives develop doubt in their abilities and self-shame.

It is the importance of toileting at this stage that makes potty training an issue that must be handled sensitively. As she begins to be able to control her anal sphincters, Becky will begin to want to use the toilet like "big people" do. If she is punished for her failures, then she will develop doubt and shame. Toilet training may be an exhaustive time for everyone involved, but it must be handled sensitively.

Freud explained it like this: The urge to empty the bowel creates tension. This tension creates conflict when Mom and Dad initiate toilet training because Becky must then choose between: (1) enjoying the pleasure of immediately emptying her bowel and therefore suffering the pain of Mom's and Dad's disapproval or (2) suffering the pain of delaying emptying her bowel and therefore enjoying Mom's and Dad's approval. If toileting is sensitively done, Becky learns to balance her personal desires (emptying her bowel) with social requirements (using the toilet). If, however, toileting is initiated before Becky is ready for it and is done in a harsh and demanding way, then Becky will develop emotional symptoms later.

Toilet training is so important to development that Freud said that there are two types of personalities based upon insensitive toilet training: anal expulsive personalities and anal retentive personalities. Anal expulsives are people who unconsciously adapted to their parental authority by becoming irresponsible, sloppy, and overindulgent. This can be thought of as a psychic expulsion of feeling. Anal retentives, on the other hand, are people who are excessively neat, clean, stubborn and narrow-minded. This can be thought of as a psychic retention of feeling. From a Freudian perspective, anal retentive and anal expulsive people are those who developed shame and doubt rather than autonomy when faced with unreasonable toilet training.

Like the Stage 1 continuum, Stage 2 can also be thought of as a continuum. This continuum must be a balance between self-expression and self-control. We already have enough people in this country running around who believe in their right of uncontrolled self-expression.

We want to produce children who balance between the two ends of the continuum. In American society, we do want a child to feel independent, but only so far as he does not infringe on the rights of others. If he has not developed the ability to feel shame and doubt when his actions are uncontrolled, then he will practice uncontrolled self-expression and be a menace to society.

How many of us have not had a child look at us and say, "I can do anything I want. I know my rights!" (And how many of us have wanted to knock him silly, clear across the floor? But thank Heavens, we controlled ourselves and didn't.) That child may (or may not) be expressing an uncontrolled sense of autonomy, unregulated by shame and doubt.

Stage 3 is the stage of development of *Initiative vs. Guilt.* This stage is from three to six years of age. While the focus at the second stage is being independent, Eriksen explained that the focus of the third stage builds upon autonomy the joy of figuring out things to do and then doing them for the sheer pleasure of it.

Whereas in Stage 2, children first learned that they could control the actions of others to some extent (I can make Mama praise me if I use the potty), at Stage 3, they increase their understanding of controlling the actions of others and of things. As part of their struggle to become independent from their parents, children at this stage become obsessed with adult roles. They try playing house, playing teacher, playing soldier, playing doctor. In the process of playing these adult roles, a child's physical skills develop in hundreds of new ways. As Molly pushes the broom, erases the chalkboard, climbs over the fence, and peers into her patient's mouth, she develops new abilities, and the clumsy three-year-old becomes an infinitely more sophisticated six-year-old.

This delightful stage is the one where Molly wants to stand on a stool beside you and help you stir the cookie batter. She wants to push the vacuum for you. She may even want to help you drive, but for Heaven's sakes, please don't let her. The streets are scary enough with teenagers driving.

Becky's guilt at this stage arises from *the difference between the level of ability needed to perform a task and her self-perceived abilities.* If she believes that she can stir the stiff cookie dough and she is unable to stir it, then she may feel guilt. If she believes that she can push the vacuum for you, but the big thing won't move, then she may feel guilt. I won't even address the issue of the car. The point here is that Becky needs lots of positive experiences if she is to become a person who takes initiative.

As in the previous two stages, we want our children's growth to fall between the two ends of the continuum, but toward the industry end. We do want people to have initiative, but we also want them to feel guilt when they overstep established, reasonable limits. For example, when Randy wants to fix the leaky garden hose, you admire his industry; but when he decides to get a tool he needs out of your toolbox without your permission, you want him to feel guilty about it.

At this point, let me make a clarifying statement about the difference between shame and guilt. Shame is external in source. We are ashamed when other people know that we have transgressed. Guilt is internal in source. Even if no one ever knows about our transgression, we can feel guilt. That is, of course, assuming that we resolved the Initiative vs. Guilt crisis somewhere on the continuum that includes guilt.

From the age of six to the age of twelve, the child negotiates the crisis of *Industry vs. Inferiority*. This focuses on the child's ability to gain recognition for performance. This performance may be social, intellectual, or physical. Whatever the activities are that are favored by a society are the activities that the child at this stage will tackle.

Since American society, as portrayed by television, places such emphasis on sports, violence, and rock music, is it any surprise that many young children begin to show interest in these things at this time? Seldom have I ever seen an academic event on television. Seldom have I seen peaceful coexistence portrayed on television. Since television provides children with a window on their world, it may be that exposure to television at this age is especially crucial.

Because the crisis at this stage requires Tomas to learn cooperation, it has been said that this stage is the most socially decisive stage. This stage marks the beginning of the work ethic, in which a sense of what is valued by his society is instilled in Tomas. At this time, if you assign tasks to Tomas that seem important and worthwhile to him, he will develop industry. Assignment of tasks that he sees as meaningless, or that are beyond his capacity to perform, will instill in him a sense of inferiority.

For example, are the boys in your cottage usually assigned to do things that seem more interesting than the things that girls are assigned to do? When Melissa views her gender as being related to the kinds of chores she does, she will begin to feel that girls are inferior to boys. Tasks should be deemed important to children doing them, if they are to contribute to a sense of industry.

Sometimes I have observed that the children in my classes who have the greatest sense of industry are those from families in which every member must contribute to the family's survival. When Melissa knows that she is responsible for taking care of Baby Ellen so that Mom can work to feed the family, then Melissa develops industry. Any child knows that taking care of the baby so Mom can make money to buy food is a chore that is important and worthy.

On the other hand, I have observed a great many middle-class children who never developed industry. Allen had no need to contribute to the family welfare; in fact, everything was done for him. He saw himself without purpose in the family structure. He was simply a consumer of the fruits of the labor of others. In addition, he was very bright, so school presented no challenge for him. Or perhaps his teachers didn't create exciting, worthy projects around which to center his studies; the studies themselves were a paragon of meaninglessness. Allen grew up feeling that doing meaningful, important things was something that was for other people, that he could not do meaningful things. This sense of inferiority led him to expect other people to continue paying his way long after he was an adult.

That leads us to the next stage of Erikson's model of psychosocial development: the crisis of *Identity vs. Identity Diffusion.* This is my favorite stage to think about, in part because adolescence is my primary age of study as a social psychologist. *Identity crisis is* the term for which Eriksen is best known. Just think, before Eriksen came along, there was no such thing as an identity crisis! There were just teenagers running around acting like real jerks without any reason for it. After Eriksen developed the notion of the identity crisis, parents could at last view this particularly tacky time as a stage which their child was going through, and not as the advent of a hideous new creature which their child had become for all time.

Identity crisis is so important that I have reserved a special chapter, the very next one, for it all by itself. Take it at this point that the identity crisis is the next stage and go on from there to look at the rest of Eriksen's work. Then stretch your legs, make a fresh cup of coffee (maybe a nice mocha), and then come back to read the identity chapter while you sip your brew.

Since we are interested in the children in our homes, I will not spend much time on the remaining three stages; however, it will be helpful to you to know what they are.

Erikson's sixth stage is the stage of *Intimacy vs. Isolation.* This is the stage of young adulthood. Here, an individual either learns to have a close, loving relationship with another, or he does not. This is why many people who put off love until after their careers are well established never do develop intimate relationships. They unintentionally resolved the crisis in favor of isolation, although they were unaware of it.

Stage seven is the crisis of *Generativity vs. Stagnation.* This runs from young adulthood to middle age. Generativity refers to the middleager's urge to pass on what she has learned to the next generation. Most people fulfill this urge primarily through raising a family. Other people have energy left over to devote to their communities or to younger colleagues. Still other people who do not have children invest all of their generative impulses into nurturing others. However, if Billy does not successfully resolve this crisis, then he feels that his life is meaningless and at a dead end.

The last stage is the crisis of *Integrity vs. Despair.* This crisis runs through old age. Erikson explained that integrity is Billy's developing a peaceful sense of satisfaction with his past. This is a spiritual concern of sorts and is contingent upon how Billy resolved his earlier life crises.

When Erikson was 92, he explained that he and his wife had come to believe that *wisdom* was the resolution of this crisis and could not be acquired without successful resolution of the earlier life crises. When you think about it, it makes perfect sense. Isn't it the old person who has a great spiritual peace about her that you think of as wise?

In this chapter, we have discussed Erikson's psychosocial stages, paying particular attention to those stages from birth through adolescence. In the next chapter we will discuss the identity crisis.

Chapter 7

THE IDENTITY CRISIS

In the last chapter, we outlined Erikson's stages of psychosocial development. In this chapter, we will examine the identity crisis more closely. In order to do this, we will also examine adolescence itself more closely.

With the arrival of puberty comes an onslaught of hormones. Parts of your body that you never gave a second thought to suddenly demand your attention. This new self-awareness causes Becky's mind to be full of self-doubt. Do you remember that Piaget taught us that adolescents are able to imagine what might be, instead of only what is? Whereas before, Becky saw herself as pretty if Mom said she was pretty, she now begins to wonder whether she might really be ugly. She spends hours in front of the mirror examining every tiny blemish. A pimple that might have gone entirely unnoticed before now receives her total examination several times a day; obsession might be a better word. "Ohmigosh," she thinks as she stares at The Thing that has grown on her face. "I am ugly! I'm not pretty at all! I'm dead-dog-down-in-the-dump ugly!"

As she negotiates her way through adolescence, Becky may move back and forth along a continuum between *I-am-pretty/I-am-ugly* and land anywhere in between. She may end up believing that she's pretty. On the other hand, she may end up believing that she is not pretty, and vow to develop other abilities that will make her attractive. For example, I recall hearing several comediennes over the years tell that they developed their funny persona because they were physically unattractive children. "I couldn't compete with the pretty girls with my looks, but I could hold my own by making people laugh," women like Phyllis Diller and Carol Burnett have said.

Some girls will care more than others about their looks. Some girls will care more than others about their schoolwork and careers. I can't imagine women, such as my heroes, Lady Jane Goodall or Diane Fossey, wasting much time on how they looked in high school. After all, when you spent most of your adult life living with great apes, how interested in good looks could you be? While I may be wrong, I would bet that while these women noticed a new blemish on their chins when they were fifteen, that it didn't demand much of their attention. I would bet that they were far more interested in getting to school and observing the snake in the biology lab.

However, the beginning stirrings of sexuality tend to make teenagers superconscious of their looks. After all, the first thing that another person judges us by is how we look. In fact, you would be amazed at how many inferences we make about another person based upon how pretty or unattractive they are.

Certainly, since time immemorial, prettiness has generally been the first characteristic which men have sought in women. As Chris-in-the-Morning on "Northern Exposure" once said, the search for the biological (and cultural) ideal is "stamped into the primal brain." After all, when a guy goes into the boys' locker room and tells the other guys that he has a date with a new girl for Friday night, what is the first thing the guys ask? Here is a hint: It is not, "Does she have a good mind?" Their question will be some derivative of, "Is she pretty?" It may be a rather crude derivative, but the basic crux of the question deals with whether her face or body meets the cultural ideal of beauty.

It is important to note here that prettiness is defined by the culture in which we live. For example, whereas thin women are considered beautiful in the U.S., soft, round women are considered beautiful in many (maybe most) other countries. One of my college students, a woman from Colombia, told me, "I have put on twenty pounds since I have been here. But it is okay with me. You see, in my country, it is the round, soft woman who is considered beautiful. Not like here in the United States where 'thin is in.'"

Subsequent to that conversation, I have considered moving to Colombia. I could have a whole nation at my feet.

While prettiness tends to be the first characteristic that men desire in women, physical prowess tends to be the first characteristic that women desire in men. There is a biological reason for this. In the early days of our evolution, when survival itself was dependent upon the physical strength of the men in the family unit, having a strong mate was essential for the survival of a woman and her children. You didn't want a saber-toothed tiger coming after you and your babies under any circumstances, but your chances were much better if you were being chased by a saber-tooth and your mate was Arnold Schwarzenegger rather than Alan Alda.

So while whether or not a girl and boy continue to be attracted to each other depends on a gazillion other characteristics, the initial attraction is generally how the body/face of the other looks. Given that, is it surprising that the identity crisis brings with it constant hypercritical examination of one's physical flaws?

In addition to "Who am I physically?" a related question in the identity crisis is, "Who am I sexually?" Some research suggests that one of every eleven Americans is gay. Recent genetic and biophysical research suggests that sexual orientation may be genetically determined. However, even teenagers who are genetically heterosexual and who grow up to be confident heterosexuals may at times during adolescence question their sexuality.

Among boys, the natural love that they feel for their close friends may worry them. "Why do I feel so close to Jim? I love him and want to hang around with him. Does that mean that I'm gay?" Many young boys engage in group sessions of masturbation. If Billy is aroused by watching other boys masturbate, he may wonder whether he is gay, even if he develops into a heterosexual. This period of wondering can be highly stressful for a young man.

On the other hand, the gay child may experience even greater trauma as he negotiates the identity crisis as he continues to find evidence supporting the notion that he is gay.

A good friend of mine in high school approached me one day. Larry was a brilliant boy, a year behind me in school, and I was sure that this "little brother" of mine had a great future ahead of him. "I have to talk to you," he said, so we got in my car and drove to the drive-in and got a soda.

"Shoot," I said.

"I don't know how to say this," he answered.

"Just spill it."

"I'm afraid I'm gay," said Larry.

I was a little startled. "Why?" I asked.

"Well," he admitted, "I find myself being sexually attracted to my best friend, Bud. For example, we're in phys ed together, and I catch myself wanting to look at him when he is undressed."

Somewhere I had read something about adolescent development, so I confidently came back with, "Oh, don't worry. That's perfectly natural for guys your age. You'll get over it."

Then he went on to tell me that I was the only girl whom he'd ever loved, and that *did* surprise me, because I had never thought of Larry in a romantic way. "Oh, you'll find the right girl some day," I said, "and that will clear up any feelings you have about me. And you'll get over these feelings about Bud. Don't worry. It's just a phase you're going through."

Now, remember that this was the 1960s, a time in which we still viewed homosexuality as abnormal, a mental disorder. I knew that Larry was a good kid and certainly no "pervert." I was sure he'd grow out of it.

Well, Larry didn't grow out of it. He went on to become a member of the gay community in a nearby town, but I don't think that he ever outgrew the sense of guilt that he had about being gay. He finally committed suicide before he ever reached twenty-five. In retrospect, I wish that I had known then what I know now. I would have told him that, statistically, 136 kids in our high school of 1500 were gay, and that gay was simply another way that some people were born.

While sexuality is an extremely important issue in identity development, there are other issues as well. "Am I a rocker, or a preppie, or a dweeb, or a greaser?" Now, to you and me, at middle age, that's a pretty easy question to answer. But if you will think back, you may remember asking yourself essentially the same question. Of course, our generations may have had different terms. In my generation, it was more like *hippie, jock,* or *egghead.* But the idea is the same. We tried on a variety of persona, sometimes changing day by day. Some days, I wore blue jeans and a sweatshirt. Other days, I wore my French beret, a turtleneck, and stretch pants. Still other days, I wore my academic and band letter sweater and a pleated skirt. Unless all my clothes were dirty and I was wearing something out of desperation, my attire announced that day's persona to the world. It is the case that our clothing, which we do wear to make a statement about who we are, is called our *exogeneous skeleton.* That means that our clothing protects us by surrounding us with our image.

Career questions must be addressed during identity crisis. Be aware that *career* and *job* are not the same thing. Career is considered to be a life-style choice, of which a job is only a part; in contrast, a job is considered to be a way to get money. For example, my public school teaching career was a different life-style from my career as a college professor. Likewise, each of these two careers have very different lifestyles from my career as a houseparent. Now, when I was working my way through college, I had a job as a bank teller. That was not a career, just a job. All it did was provide me with money.

It is during the identity crisis that we see how the resolutions of the earlier crises contribute to the development of identity. A teenager who has successfully negotiated the earlier crises of developing the ability to trust others, a sense of independence, initiative, and a desire to take problems head on, is pointed in the direction of positively resolving her identity crisis.

The opposite of identity is *identity diffusion*. Identity diffusion means that Billy is unable to properly establish his identity through consolidating his feelings about who he is. Erikson explained that identity diffusion, or negative identity, often takes the form of a scornful or snobbish hostility. This hostility is directed toward the roles that the person's family or community expect him to fill. If the family expects the identity diffused teen to be a good student, then the teen looks down his nose at good students. If the community expects the teen to be a good citizen, then the teen looks down his nose at good citizens. If the family expects the teen to be a hard worker, then he looks down his nose at people who work hard.

This is the typical rebel without a cause. Billy doesn't can't come to a resolution about who he is, so he's just going to be against everything. His parents are dumbfounded by the fact that Billy screeches that all adults are narrow-minded and bigoted when they don't approve of his purple, spiked hair, yet he narrow-mindedly and bigotedly berates them because they wear conventional middle-aged haircuts. Ditto for his choice in music, heroes, values, and political ideas.

However, Eriksen explained that a teenager may delay dealing with the identity crisis and take a *psychosocial moratorium*. Do you remember that Eriksen spent some time roaming about European cities considering art as a career? He later considered this a moratorium and believed that moratoria are healthy. He said that the moratorium could be used to gain new experiences and perspectives on life and that these are likely to contribute to a very positive outcome when the moratorium ends.

James Marcia built upon Eriksen's work. He interviewed male teenagers about their views toward sexuality, religion, values, and careers. Based upon these interviews, he found that there are four identity statuses: *identity achievement, identity foreclosure, identity moratorium,* and *identity diffusion.*

Identity achievement adolescents have made a number of choices about their lives. For example, Billy may have determined that he is a confident heterosexual male, yet he may not know what career he wants to pursue. He may know that he is committed to the religion of his parents but not know where he stands on value issues that he does not believe relate directly to his religion. He has made these decisions based upon his own personal choice and not because he has been coerced into them.

Like identity achievers, identity foreclosers also know who they are. But unlike identity achievers, the child who has identity foreclosure does not make his own decisions. He simply accepts the decisions that others have made for him. A young man once said to me, "All the men in my family are in the family lumberyard. I never wanted to work here, but that's who we are. That's what we do. So I work in the lumberyard. Finished. Settled."

I asked him what it was that he really wanted to do. "Be a photojournalist," he replied. "But that's nonsense. Just dreaming. Because we're a lumberyard family." He looked dreamily past me. "But I do have some really nice shots.... And I even won a prize in a contest once!"

While I don't know how many people are identity foreclosed, I suspect it's a pretty good percentage of the population. The tragic downside of this is that many people live their lives out never doing what they really want to do, and much real talent may be wasted. On the upside, identity foreclosers are able to avoid the chaos of the identity crisis. When you already know who you are because you succumbed to your parents and let them decide that for you, you don't have to agonize about it.

Marcia's third identity type is the identity moratorium type. Like Erikson, Marcia agrees that this child has not made any decisions yet. This child may seem distracted a good deal of the time, the typical, "Earth to Billy, Billy to Earth" kid. Marcia also explains that the moratorium person often has highly intense, yet short-lived relationships. Today, Billy is wildly excited by the idea of being an artist and living alone in a musty garret in Paris, but tomorrow, he may be wildly excited by the idea of being an accountant and marrying Elaine and living in Ohio. He may also be wildly excited by a life-style like joining the Hell's Angels and living on the open road with a woman named Hot Mama, but he will probably drop that nonsense pretty quickly and achieve a more socially approved persona.

The final type does not achieve a persona. The identity diffused adolescent is well described by Erikson earlier, but Marcia added that the diffuser is impulsive, scattered, not goal-oriented, and unable to make a commitment either to a career or another person. This is the individual who jumps around from job to job and relationship to relationship. This person quits every job because, "They weren't fair to me," "They didn't treat me right," or "They didn't pay me what I was worth." He will be intolerant and immature in his treatment of others.

I want to note here that Gilligan, the feminist theorist who gave us the model of morality based upon caring and responsibility, argues that women undergo an additional crisis at this time: the crisis of intimacy. Whereas Eriksen places the intimacy crisis in young adulthood rather than in adolescence, Gilligan contends that teenage girls must settle the intimacy crisis concurrently with the identity crisis in adolescence. Any houseparent who has been the confidant of a teenage girl knows how intense her love relationships are. Colette will spend hour after hour dreaming of being married to Rocky; Rocky loves Colette, too, but is really more interested in playing football after school than in dreaming about Colette. That's why so many girls sit home and wait for the phone to ring instead of going out with their friends. Of course, these days more girls call boys, so perhaps they will feel freer to go on out with their friends instead of waiting by the phone.

Next, I want to talk about the work of David Elkind and how he helped us understand more about the identity crisis.

In 1963, David Elkind began to extend the work of Piaget. Central to his notion of adolescent development was the idea of *the grass is greener* thinking. As you supposed, the grass is greener refers to the ability to see how things could be, instead of how things actually are. Elkind suggested that this is at the roots of much of teenagers' argumentativeness. Whereas when she was a younger child, Mona couldn't conceive that things don't have to be as they are, as a teenager, she now can understand that things can be changed. (Except for death and taxes. We're pretty much stuck with those.)

For example, before Mona developed grass-is-greener thinking, she never questioned cottage rules. Bedtime was at nine and that was that. Finito. The end. Finished. But once she developed the ability to think about the way things could be, in addition to the way things are, presto chango, she begins to argue with us. "But I'm fifteen years old. I shouldn't have to go to bed when the littler kids do. I'm doing okay in school, so if I want to stay up late to watch David Letterman, I ought to be able to do it."

Better yet, she may say, "Well, in our cottage, we only have fruit or yogurt for a bedtime snack. But over in Lee Cottage, they get chocolate cake. So why can't we have chocolate cake? We want chocolate cake, too. If they can have it, we can have it." Or try this one on for size. "Lee Cottage has a nice housemother. Why can't we have nice housemother like her, instead of you?"

This particularly relates to the identity crisis as Mona thinks about who she is as compared to who other people are. "I have cellulite on my thighs," thinks Mona. "Joy doesn't have cellulite. I'd rather be Joy than me." She then begins to compare every other feature of her own self to Joy. This comparing of self provides an important part of identity development. "I'm not as pretty as Joy, but my legs are nicer than hers. And I'm not funny like she is, but I'm smarter." As Mona considers these things, she may commit to decisions to change herself to make herself more like the person she wishes to be. "I could change my makeup and do it more like Joy does hers. And I could work at being funny."

Piece by piece, Mona examines her being and compares it to a personal ideal. Sometimes she'll find herself comparing favorably to the ideal. More often, she'll find herself falling short. As she either accepts these shortcomings or embarks on campaigns to change them, she further develops a sense of who she is.

The next thing that relates to the identity crisis is *dispositional thinking*. This means that whereas before, when thinking about herself, Mona would think, "I have brown hair," or "I am in sixth grade," she now thinks about herself (and others) in abstract terms. She will now think, "I'm an honest person," referring to a personality disposition, instead of a simplistic description, such as hair color.

This dispositional thinking will be very complex. Mona will be able to view the disposition from a variety of perspectives and examine it in critical, minute detail: "I'm an honest person, but I'm not an idiot. I'll lie to save my skin if I have to. But under most conditions, I'll tell the truth and even take a punishment if I'm standing up for one of my friends."

So now, instead of thinking of herself merely as someone who has brown hair, Mona can begin to examine her complex identity in very complex ways.

The next information that Elkind gave us that relates to adolescent identity is *role taking and perspectivistic thinking*. This means that now, Mona can take someone else's role in a situation and can see herself from that person's perspective. Before, either she didn't think at all about what other people thought or she believed that they thought what she thought. When she always got the biggest piece of cake, she thought, "People think I'm smart, because I always manage to get the biggest piece," or she didn't think at all about what they thought. Now, however, she can see her behavior from the perspective of other people. "People think I'm a hog because I always try to get the biggest piece," she thinks. Elkind said that this ability to role take and engage in perspectivistic thinking is the cornerstone of adolescent development.

Many children who have behavior problems, particularly those children we get in basic care, have difficulty in role taking. They have never developed the ability to see a situation the way another person sees it. Travis, the boy with the BB gun that I alluded to in the introduction, was just such a person.

One day, my husband and I came home from school to find a BB gun on the kitchen table. Travis was our seventeen-year-old foster son, so we knew that he must have bought it. I didn't necessarily approve of BB guns, but my husband argued that having a BB gun is something that most boys in our part of the country did at a much younger age and that it was perfectly appropriate for Travis to buy one. Since Travis had been in a group home from the time he was seven until he came to live with us at seventeen, he had never owned a BB gun.

When Travis came home from school, my husband said, "I know that you're real excited about having your first BB gun. But you have to be careful; owning any kind of gun is a big responsibility. Use it far away from the animals and be sure that you don't shoot holes in the windows of the barn."

Travis, who couldn't any more see our perspective than a turkey can fly a kite, grinned at us, walked to the door, opened it up, and with one foot inside the kitchen and the other on the porch, shot the barn window full of BB holes. Then he turned to us and grinned sheepishly, as though we would think, "Isn't he a cute little rascal!"

Travis thought it would be a cute thing to do. He simply couldn't see our perspective on the issue. He seemed truly, utterly dumbfounded when we were angry.

Adolescent egocentricism is the next concept that Elkind gave us that we need to think about as we discuss identity development. Adolescent egocentricism has two main characteristics, *the imaginary audience* and *the personal fable*. Adolescent egocentricism explains why each teenager thinks that s/he is the most important person in the world.

Before she developed perspectivistic thinking, Mona didn't realize that other people had perspectives which were different from her perspective. She thought that everyone thought that she was smart for taking the biggest piece of cake. Now that she has perspectivistic thinking, she realizes that other people may have vastly different perspectives from hers. But here's the rub. Follow me closely.

Elkind explains that development occurs on two planes: vertical and horizontal. First, we enter a new level of development. That growth is like a sapling growing straight up but without any branches. This is vertical growth. So at this point, I can sit next to the sapling, but I don't have any shade, because the tree is a tall stick without any branches. After the tree is at the new height for a while, it spreads its branches. Now, I have shade under the tree. That spreading of the branches is horizontal growth, a maturing of the tree at its new height.

In the same way, Mona has experienced vertical growth in her abilities: she can now think perspectivisticly. However, her abilities are immature. She needs horizontal growth which comes from experience with using her new abilities, experience which comes with time and intellectual/social growth. So, Mary uses perspectivistic thinking immaturely. What that translates into is this: Mary realizes that other people may have perspectives different from her own, but she thinks that those other people's perspectives are centered on her!

By believing that all people have their attention centered on her, Mona has created what Elkind calls the imaginary audience. The reason that Mona believes everyone's attention is centered on her is due to what Elkind calls the personal fable.

A variety of personal fables exist. Personal fables involve the belief that one is unique and special. The belief that she is unique and special leads Mona to believe that no one has ever been as happy, as sad, or as in love as she is. Since no one has ever experienced these feelings to the extent Mona experiences them, no one in the world can possibly understand what she is feeling.

Personal fables may also involve the belief that we are destined for greatness. A student of mine in past years regularly demonstrated her belief in the personal fable of being destined for greatness. Although Debbie was a talented writer for a high school student, she didn't apply herself. Because of her personal fable, she said that she was going to write a best-selling novel before high school graduation and be a millionaire by the time she enrolled at an Ivy League school. I warned Debbie that if she wanted to be a writer, she had to write every day and to keep her grades up so that she could get into a prestigious school. But she didn't listen, and she sloughed off her high school years. By the time she graduated, the great American novel remained unwritten, the million dollars remained unmade, and the Ivy League school remained unattainable.

The most interesting story of an imaginary audience that I know of was told to me by Tracy, a thirteen-year-old who was in my room during my second year of teaching. One day, Tracy told me that he had to talk to me in private after school. I agreed to meet with him.

When he arrived, he confided to me that he sometimes felt as though he were the only real person alive. He felt as though all places and things were sets and props on a giant stage and that they were dismantled as soon as he was out of view. All people were robots, set about by Martians, or some other such creatures, in order to see how Tracy, the ultimate guinea pig, would respond to them. He said:

> I even feel like you are a robot, and I feel stupid for telling you all this because you already know it. You already know the script, and you know what you are supposed to say, and as soon as I leave, this room will be dismantled and you will be turned off.

As a young teacher, my first impression was that Tracy was mentally ill. (He was, after all, the child who had hidden his dead dog in the closet because he was afraid his mother would be mad at him because the dog had been run over.) Yet as I thought about Tracy's confession for a few days, I remembered something startling. I, too, had suffered from the same delusion as a young teen. The memories came flooding back; giant unseen beings had constructed an elaborate stage upon which they tested my behavior by means of expertly crafted robots. My parents were robots. My teachers were robots. Everyone was a robot! I, alone, was a human being, and I was constantly observed by the unseen beings. I, too, had believed that each stage was torn down and erected again as needed. And I wasn't mentally ill. (Then again, I had never hidden a dead dog in the closet.) I began to realize that Tracy probably wasn't any crazier than I was at that age.

When the attention of everyone is on you, it's no wonder that you worry all the time about your identity. Holy cow! You could never measure up to what other people expect of the center of the psychological universe!

If Tracy was the most interesting case of adolescent egocentricism, I know Dale was the most persistent.

Dale came to me as a fourteen-year-old. Throughout our four years together, *every time* he would see me talking quietly with another adult, he would confront me as soon as I was alone.

"Tell me what were you two saying about me!" he would demand. At first I was surprised. As this behavior continued over the next several months, I became alarmed. Finally, I learned about adolescent egocentricism and became amused. I wondered just how long Dale would continue thinking that he was the center of all my (and everyone else's) thoughts and was sort of sad to see it gradually end when he turned eighteen.

In this chapter, we have closely examined the resolution of the identity crisis, the fifth of Erikson's psychosocial stages. We have devoted this extensive amount of time to our discussion of adolescent identity, because this is the stage at which we as houseparents will face the toughest battles. Even other people's kids who have been relatively easy to raise as children will make us want to kill them at some time during their teenage years. Knowing what makes teenagers act like they do should help us keep our cool.

In the next chapter, we will discuss self-concept and self-esteem.

Chapter 8

IMPROVING CHILDREN'S SELF–ESTEEM

In the last chapter, we discussed the development of identity. Another way of saying identity is *self-concept*. An important part of self-concept is *self-esteem*. Whereas self-concept (or identity) is who we see ourself as being, self-esteem is how good we feel about who we are. In this chapter, we will look at self-esteem and appropriate ways that houseparents can increase a child's self-esteem. (The key word here is *appropriate*.)

Self-esteem is comprised of two psychological processes: *self-worth* and *self-evaluation*. Self-worth refers to a sense of security and feeling of worth as a person. "We love you not because of what you do but just because you're you" is a phrase we often hear parents use which promotes self-worth. Self-worth is not tied to any situation; it's a general feeling of "I'm loved and special just because I'm me."

On the other hand, self-evaluation is a process of consciously judging one's social importance. This is tied to situations: If Tony believes that being a left fielder is important and he evaluates his performance as a left fielder as good, then his self-esteem is enhanced. On the other hand, if he believes that being a left fielder is important but he evaluates his performance as a left fielder as bad, then his self-esteem is damaged. On yet another hand, if he doesn't believe that being a left fielder is important, then it doesn't matter whether he evaluates his performance as good or bad; he doesn't see this as socially significant.

Children who come to us in basic care are particularly at risk to have low self-esteem from both low self-worth and low self-evaluation. Who could have poorer self-worth than a child whose parents have abandoned her, neglected her, or abused her? "I'm not even worth being a mom or dad to," Teena thinks. "Who could possibly love me?" Probably every child who comes to us in basic care has poor self-esteem.

As David builds a concept of who he is, the question arises: what value does he place on the things he is? David may first and foremost see himself as a Boys' Rancher (read *group home resident*). How good does David feel about being a Boys' Rancher? Probably not very. In our home, new boys might be proud of the term, because our ranch was beautiful. Two sets of houseparents and sixteen boys lived in each half-million-dollar cottage. The cottages were sprawling brick ranch houses with greatrooms which held a fireplace and looked like ski lodges. For a boy who had lived in a rundown shack, the initial idea of being a Boys' Rancher was pretty appealing.

But once the new wore off, the boys couldn't help but learn little by little that Boys' Ranchers were not thought well of in the community. "You don't want anything to do with him. He's a Boys' Rancher," or "I hope I don't get any more Boys' Ranchers in my class," were comments that boys couldn't help but overhear at school or in the mall on Saturday nights. These comments damaged a child's general self-worth. "I'm worthless. Nobody wants me," is a generalized feeling that many of our kids have.

In contrast to self-worth, self-evaluation is based upon specific successes and failures of valued abilities. Boys who were good athletes at our home had high esteem about that, but boys who couldn't make the team had low self-esteem about that.

However, a child could be very good at something and not value it at all. For example, a boy could be a good student but not value that because scholarship was not valued by his peers.

Mercy. What a mess.

So many of the decisions that a child must make are contingent upon his self-esteem. For example, he has to decide whether he has the ability to try out for football. "Am I strong enough? Fast enough?" If he values football (and I think that the majority of young men probably do) and if his self-esteem is low because he doesn't think he is strong enough to make the team, then his low self-esteem has prevented him from even giving it a try.

If he wants to go to college but doesn't think that he is smart enough to pass the required high school math courses, then his low self-esteem in that area has blocked him entirely out of pursuing a collegiate career.

If he thinks that he is a person who can't make friends, then his low self-esteem in this area will prevent him from even trying.

Do you have a child in your cottage who won't ever try anything new? I'll bet it's because he has low self-esteem and is afraid to try.

The origins of self-esteem are largely based on the interaction between a child and her social experiences. If Janey's mom has screeched at her in drunken rage, "You're no damn good! I wish I'd never had you!" then

Janey learns that she is of no worth as a person. And after all, if you're not good enough for your own mom to want you, how could you possibly be of any value at all?

Only as Janey experiences a gazillion interactions in which she is told that she is a valuable, worthwhile person will her self-worth begin to improve. Even a gazillion times might not do the trick.

As opposed to self-worth, which is a general feeling of self and is not tied to situations, Janey's self-evaluations are tied to specific situations in which her interactions with her social world determine her self-esteem. If Janey values being a cook and she tries to help you make cornbread, she is testing whether or not she is good at this thing that she wants as part of her self-concept. If you say, "Janey! You did a wonderful job!" and praise her at dinner in front of the family, then she develops high self-esteem about her ability to be a cook. If, on the other hand, you say, "Janey! You just made a mess! Get out of the kitchen and let me get dinner finished!" then her self-esteem is lowered.

On the other hand, if Janey does not value being a gardener and you scold her for not being careful in her weeding, then her self-esteem is not likely to suffer. "So I can't weed," she thinks. "Big deal." That's the way I would view being able to lob a tennis ball. You can tell me all day that I'm a failure at tennis, and I'll still sleep like a baby tonight. But don't tell me that I'm a poor teacher, or my self-esteem will drop, because while I don't value playing tennis, I do value teaching. Under these circumstances, neither Janey's nor my self-esteem will be damaged.

A houseparent's acceptance and positive evaluation is crucial to the development of positive self-esteem in Boys' Ranchers. In fact, social acceptance in general and self-acceptance are closely combined.

It is important to note that self-worth and self-evaluation are not entirely independent of one another. If I tell Peter over and over that he is a poor student, athlete, musician, poet, swimmer, whatever, then the accumulation of these negative evaluations will probably result in a negative self-worth. The reverse is true as well. This is why an integral part of every children's home should be the opportunity for children to receive many successes of many kinds every day.

I think it's interesting that many children who are in special education have been found to have very high self-esteem. This poses an interesting question: How could a person who is unable to perform so many essential and valued living skills feel so good about themselves? The answer is probably that special education teachers and parents of children with disabilities focus so much on, "You are special just because you are you. It doesn't matter that you can't do (whatever) like other kids do. You're great just like you are!" Therefore, kids who have disabilities often have great self-worth which overrides situational self-evaluation.

One time when self-esteem is particularly important is when a serious or urgent decision must be made. At these times, self-concept pops into the front of our minds. "Somebody has to stop that bully from harassing my little sister. Am I brave enough to stand up to him? Do people think I'm a nerd and so they'll laugh at me? Will people make fun of me if I step in between them because I'm skinny and weak?"

Based upon this notion, when a child has what he considers an important decision, we should begin feeding him positive evaluations. "You should try out for the baseball team. You are quick and you have great eye-hand coordination." Of course, if he is slow and can't catch a watermelon with a laundry basket, you probably don't want to set him up for failure. Instead, try and help him devalue that activity in order that he won't see his failure to make the team as important. After all, I've lived a pretty good life without being able to play tennis.

While I'm at it, let me talk about schoolwork for a moment. If a child has serious irremediable learning problems, then we need to be like those special education teachers and parents of children with disabilities. Sometimes, the kindest thing that I have ever done for a high schooler who could not read even a second grade book was to say, "Look, I know your teachers have been trying for ten years to teach you to read. And I know that you've been trying for that long. So let's give it up. Reading is nice, but it's not the end of the world. Lots of people have gone on and done just fine and could never read a word. What *is* important is the things that you *can* do and that's what we're going to focus on. You're a hard worker and you're going to be a wonderful husband and father and provider and friend. Those are the important things in life. So forget about reading and let's get on with the things that you *can* do with your life."

A psychologist by the name of Coopersmith tells us that of the conditions that we as houseparents need to create in our homes in order to develop children's sense of self-worth, these three are the most important: *parental warmth, clearly defined limits,* and *respectful treatment.*

Parental warmth refers to a nurturing, loving attitude. While the father's role as a nurturer is extremely important too, the mother's attitude toward the child seems to be the more important of the two. It's a tough break that almost all of our children come to us critically lacking in mother warmth. It creates untold problems for them. In fact, a number of psychologists believe that many children who do not experience warmth from their mothers, or who have that relationship seriously disturbed before their second birthdays, will go on to become *sociopaths* —people who do not have a conscience. These scientists say that this disruption in the mother-child bond produces children who never learn to love, and that unless you learn to love, you never learn to feel guilt. If you can't feel guilt, you don't have a conscience.

The most challenging kids that we as houseparents, foster parents, and direct care providers ever work with are kids with conduct disorders, the term we often use for kids who go on to be diagnosed as sociopaths after they turn seventeen. (No one under seventeen can be diagnosed as a sociopath.) Casey was such a kid. His mom had abandoned him when he was one year old. Casey had been a resident in a number of group home settings. He had been kicked out of his last group home. He had been caught molesting a houseparent's eight-year-old daughter. He was surprisingly open with me about it. "I knew it was wrong, but it felt good and I wanted to do it."

"What do you mean that you knew it was wrong?" I asked.

"Well, you go to jail if you get caught messing around that way with little girls."

Uh huh, I thought. Kohlberg's Level 1: pleasure-pain. Do what feels good, or don't do it if it will bring you pain.

"Would you do it again if you had the chance and could be sure that you wouldn't get caught?" I asked.

"Yeah," he admitted.

You can't say much for his conscience, but you gotta admit, he was honest.

Parental warmth, and particularly mother warmth, is so crucial that without it, a baby will die. *Marasmus* is the term that we give to babies who wither and die from lack of maternal warmth. Do you remember the babies in orphanages in Romania that stared back at us from behind the bars of their cribs after the fall of the Ceausescu regime? These babies were tiny for their ages because, although they were fed and clothed, they were not held, and rocked, and cuddled.

I would like to think that direct care providers who were responsible for those Romanian babies were the exception rather than the rule in group child care, but I don't think they were. As a houseparent, I had the opportunity to share cottages with other houseparents, and I had ample opportunity to observe other houseparents with their charges. I saw very little warmth in the interactions between many houseparents and the majority of their kids. Interactions of these houseparents and their residents were more like those between supervisors and employees than between loving parents and their children. Housemoms or dads who were nurturing and loving were set upon by their kids like a beehive on a honey tree. You could feel the love radiate from them. But these people were in the minority. The majority reserved their parental warmth for their own biological children. Others had no warmth for anyone. Have you found unnurturing houseparents in your group home?

It's not too surprising to me that peoples whose culture provides for prolonged contact between a mother's and her child's skin typically are very peaceful cultures. I have heard that among Alaskan Inuit people, the baby is tucked inside the mother's parka next to her skin for warmth until he is two years old. Children of certain other groups ride in a sling against their mother's chest until they are nearly two. This constant mother presence, this uninterrupted mother touch, creates peaceful souls that we don't promote in our own culture.

When I taught school, I tried to touch every child every day. When I was a housemother, I tried to touch every child every day. Even as a university professor, I try to touch every student at least twice a month. That's not often, but do you know what? Many of my college students tell me that they really feel that I care about them as individuals, not merely as members of my class. I think that has to have something to do with my touching them. So touch is a really powerful tool.

It makes me sick that our society has reached a point in which adults are afraid to touch children that are not their own. "Our teachers' association drills into us at every meeting, 'Don't touch kids! Don't touch kids!'" a young woman told me some time back. I shook my head. It's a sad commentary on the state of our civilization when we've reached the point where people who spend their lives raising other people's kids have to be afraid to give those kids the touching that we all so desperately need.

The second condition that promotes self-worth in a home or cottage is clearly defined limits. This is one that we seldom have trouble with as houseparents. The rules are usually set down by the agency and we simply enforce them. That is even more true for direct care providers in ward-type institutions. But it's not so simple for foster parents, since they have the advantage of living in their own homes and making their own rules.

What is important here is that most of our kids come from homes where limits weren't clearly defined. Today, Mom might say, "You're Mama's grown up girl" and give you a swig of her beer and a drag off her reefer, but tomorrow she might say, "Whaddya mean going outside in the back yard without my permission? You don't decide what you do around here! I make the decisions in this house!" and whack you for it.

It makes me think of an experiment in which a mouse was placed in a box. The floor of the front half of the box would shock the mouse when he stepped on it. The floor of the back of the mouse did not shock. This mouse was no dummy. He learned PDQ not to step on the floor of the front half of the cage.

Then, however, the researcher electrified both halves of the cage floor, but only turned on the juice at intervals. The poor mouse never knew when he was going to be shocked, where. He turned into a raving maniac before long and became a lump of quivering flesh on the floor of the cage, because he couldn't figure out where his limits were. One minute it was okay to be in the back half of the cage. The next minute it wasn't. Ditto the front half. Poor Mousie. Poor kids that live in homes like that.

Beth told me about living in such a home.

> Dad had all these weird rules off and on, and I couldn't keep up with them. Like, he had this weird thing about the toilet paper roll being put in the toilet paper holder the "right" way. The paper had to drop down from the back instead of the front. But sometimes me and the other kids forgot. I mean, who's thinking about which way you put on the roll of toilet paper when you run out and somebody has to bring you some? But anyway, he usually didn't notice, but every once in a while, maybe once a month, he'd get loaded and then beat up on somebody because the TP was on backward.

While it's important to set clearly defined limits (and most of us houseparents don't have any problem with that), here's where we do have problems: treating kids with respect.

Respectful treatment, the third of the conditions that lead a child to develop self-worth, is often forgotten by us as houseparents when a child breaks a rule. It's easy to get into the "I gotcha!" syndrome when we catch a kid breaking a rule. We need to keep rules consistent, but we need to treat children with respect, even when we catch them in the act of breaking a rule.

When we were houseparents, my husband, Kelvin, stood out from the rest of the adults on the ranch, because he never had a moment's trouble with the boys. I had some trouble, and many houseparents had constant trouble, but Kelvin never had a problem. One day, I had a run-in with a boy whom I ordered to do the dishes. He told me to "go piss up a rope." I was ticked.

"Do you know what you're doing wrong?" Kelvin asked me. I told him I did not.

He said, "The key to working with these boys is respect. I treat them like I respect them. You and most of the other houseparents don't. That's why they respect me and they don't respect most of the rest of you."

"I *do* respect the boys," I argued.

"You don't act like it," he said. "The most important thing on God's green earth to a young man is saving face. I learned that the hard way during my years as a cop in downtown Kansas City. If you treat kids with respect and show it, especially by allowing them to save face, then they'll treat you with respect."

"But I didn't make anyone lose face," I said. "I don't understand."

Kelvin explained. "A teenage boy desperately wants to be an adult. He thinks, 'If it walks like a duck, and looks like a duck, and quacks like a duck, it is a duck. I walk like a man, and look like a man, and talk like a man; therefore, I am a man.' But here you go treating him like a child. You tell him, 'Don't this and do do that and don't even think about doing the other.' By coming on like you're the big authority and he has to obey you, you set yourself up for failure. He loses face publicly if his peers see him taking orders from you. He even loses face privately if his peers aren't around. He's thinking, 'I'm just a little boy, and Mama has to tell me what to do. I only thought I was a man.' You've embarrassed him. That's a terrible thing for a kid."

I knew that embarrassment was a terrible thing for a teenager. I had read once that adolescents feared embarrassment almost equally to the death of their own parents, and since I was only a houseparent, I knew that this was not a good situation for me to be in.

"Well, how can I allow a boy to save face and still get our chores done?" I asked.

"If you treat a boy like you would a friend, with respect, he'll do most anything you ask. You wouldn't tell your friend, Anna, 'Get in there and wash those dishes right now!' You'd say, 'Hey Anna, I sure need to get these dishes done. Would you come help me, please?' And you wouldn't stand off like an overseer of slaves; you'd jump in and work together. That's where you and most of the other houseparents screw up. You've got this mind-set like you're overseers and these kids are slaves. You don't show them any respect, so they don't give you any in return."

I always hate it when I am wrong and Kelvin is right, but I have to admit that he was right and I was. . . . Well, he was right.

So right away I did an experiment. I started treating each boy in the same respectful and loving way that I treated my friends, and I seldom ever had another problem. The boys saved face and the chores got done. It was just a matter of a little thing called respect. How simple. How odd that I didn't figure it out for myself.

If parental warmth, clearly defined limits, and respectful treatment are the conditions that lead a child to see herself as someone of worth, then what are the best ways of raising a child's self-esteem?

Coopersmith researched this question, too, and came up with the following recommendations for raising a child's self-esteem: *seeing that the child experiences plenty of successes, filling her with wholesome ideas, encouraging her,* and *helping her build her defenses against the things that would rob her of her self-esteem.*

We have already talked at length about providing successful experiences for children, but I want to make one more comment about that before we go on. Providing the opportunity for kids to succeed at things they value is a lot of work on their caretakers. When we first became houseparents, I was surprised that there weren't more programs going on which would provide successes for the boys. Oh, there were plenty of programs *on paper,* but many of them were not up and running. We had a beautifully equipped wood shop that stayed locked for want of someone to agree to supervise it every day. We had a fine craft room equipped with every kind of leather tool you can imagine, but it stayed off limits for want of an adult to be in charge. We did have a ceramics class on Saturday mornings thanks to a darling little old lady volunteer. We had a parade group that rode horses in local parades, but the rest of the time, the horses were unused. Since we had lots of room to ride and were only a mile or so from BLM public lands, I was surprised that houseparents didn't take boys riding every weekend. I was also surprised to find that the professional quality roping arena was never used. We also had a pool, which was used pretty frequently, but since an adult had to be in charge, it wasn't used on a regular schedule. And we had a terrific gym, which was used most every day.

When we arrived and I began to realize that many of these facilities that I had assumed were being used regularly were not, I thought that it must be due to houseparents' fear of liability. And that may have been part of it. But what I began to realize as time went on was that supervising all those programs was a hell of a lot of work, and a lot of houseparents were burned out and just didn't want to do anything that they didn't have to do. So boys were denied the opportunity for the day in and day out successes that they needed in these areas.

The next strategy that Coopersmith gave us was filling kids with ideas. That means talking with them. Day in and day out. All the time. And you know that I'm not talking about giving them orders or asking them questions like, "Are you finished with your homework?" That doesn't count. I mean talking like families used to do before our homes were invaded by television, videocassette recorders, personal stereos, and video games. I'm talking about back in the fifties, when people really, truly talked to their kids. And kids really, truly talked to their parents. Talked about all kinds of things. Talked all the time.

I know it gets tiring talking to kids after a while. But if we want to do a good job raising other people's kids, then we gotta do it. We gotta talk, and we gotta listen. That's all there is to it.

When I was growing up, dinnertime was when our family gathered to talk. Off went the TV and radio. We had Mom's and Dad's full attention and they had ours. "Tell us what happened at school today," was the soup course, and dessert was whatever we wanted to talk about that we hadn't gotten around to yet. I really, truly knew that my parents were interested in my life.

One day, when I was teaching high school, we were reading the young adult classic novel, *Mr. and Mrs. Bojo Jones* by Ann Head, in our unit on learning about marriage. In the book, July and Bojo are quarrelling over the different ways that they think Independence Day should be celebrated. July's family celebrated Independence Day one way, and Bojo's celebrated it another. In discussing this, we started talking about how our families did mealtimes. I naively assumed that all or at least most of the kids in my class ate dinner as a family talking around the table, as we had when I was growing up, and as my husband and I continue to do. Was I ever surprised.

Not one of the eight children in the discussion group ate dinner as a family, around a table, TV turned off, discussing each person's day. One boy said that he ate on the screened-in back porch while the rest of the family ate on TV trays in the living room around the tube. Another said that he ate in his room, and each person in his family helped themselves to whatever was on the stove when they got hungry and ate wherever their favorite spot was. The closest we came to a family meal was the student who said his family all sat together around the TV while they ate.

If I could make one change in America, I would shut off every damn TV in the country and make all parents and their children sit around a table together at mealtime and talk to each other.

So talk with your kids. Talk talk talk talk talk talk talk talk talk. And then talk some more.

Number three was encouraging kids. Everybody needs a little encouragement. You need it. I need it. Other people's kids need it worse than we do. We've got some age and experience. They don't have either and they've got plenty of reason to be discouraged. So become a cheerleader for your kids.

My friend, Crystal, has always been my cheerleader. Whenever I cooked up a wild scheme, she was there cheering for me. One day she gave me a short little book called *The Balcony People,* by Joyce Landorf. I was puzzled. Then I read the book and understood. Your balcony people are the people that always stand in the balcony when you are on stage and clap and cheer wildly and yell *"BRAVO!"* for you. That's what Crystal had always done for me. Clap, and cheer wildly and yell bravo for me. That's what our kids need us to do for them.

Last of all, Coopersmith says that we must help children build defenses against onslaughts on their self-esteem. One way that we can do that is to help them learn to discount the opinions of people who attack them. When Teresa comes home crying, saying that some girl at school won't invite her to a party because she's "girls' town trash," help her learn to consider the source. It's not easy to teach a child to discount those who devalue him, but we have to keep at it.

This notion of helping build a child's defenses against things that would rob her of her self-esteem is what makes many African Americans argue against letting white foster parents adopt African American children who are in their care. "White people can't get a child ready to stand up against the prejudice that African American people still face in this country. Only another black person can do that" is the argument used by people against transracial adoptions.

Before bringing this chapter to a close, I want to talk about the dangers of developing too much self-esteem in kids. While it is less likely to develop too much self-esteem in our kids than it is in kids who live at home, it can be done.

William Damon, a professor at Brown University, warns against overstressing self-worth (as opposed to self-evaluation). He cautions that rather than telling kids, "You're wonderful, just because you're you," we should spend more time helping kids learn the skills, virtues, and values which would lead to positive self-evaluation. Repeatedly telling a kid that he is wonderful, and that telling him that without it being tied to what he does, creates a child who becomes unhealthily egocentric.

Said Damon in an article he wrote in 1991:

> Beyond its roots in the excessive child-centeredness of the current epoch, our homage to self-esteem also fuels the imbalance in a powerful way. When we tell children that the most important thing in the world is how highly they think of themselves, we clearly are telling them that they are at the center of the universe....
>
> By contributing further to the already child-centered orientation of Western culture, this emphasis can push a child toward a socially insensitive narcissism. In this way, it can impair the child's character growth. (p. 38)

Damon says that when a child believes that she is the center of the universe, then she learns to care more about her own feelings and desires than about the feelings and desires of other people. He continues:

> [Children] come to ignore the guidance and feedback of others because they have never learned to value it. They establish no firm base for respecting others, including the important adults in their lives. In the long run, they learn to act as their own moral self-referent, which of course is not morality at all.... Without an objective moral referent beyond themselves, children cannot acquire a stable sense of right and wrong. (p. 39)

Damon uses the example of the older brother who pushes his younger sister off of her bike. The parents see the incident, but the boy argues that he hasn't done anything wrong. After all, who cares what Mom and Dad think? The boy is the most important person in the world, and all that matters is what he thinks and wants.

With this warning to plant self-esteem improvement within the realm of self-evaluation ("You really helped me out by clearing off the table. You are great for doing that!") rather than in generalized global statements ("You are great, just because you're you!"), we will leave the topic of increasing self-esteem in your other people's kids.

In this chapter, we have discussed self-esteem and some strategies for raising children's self-esteem. We have also discussed a warning about telling kids that they are wonderful without tying that to positive behaviors. In the next chapter, we will discuss motivation and how we can motivate other people's kids to do better in school and at home.

Chapter 9

MOTIVATING KIDS TO BE RESPONSIBLE AND HAVE SELF-CONTROL

In the last chapter, we discussed ways of raising the self-esteem of kids who have poor self-esteem, as most of our kids do. In this chapter, we are going to talk about ways of motivating kids, or getting them to be responsible.

How much of your time do you spend trying to get other people's kids to be responsible? Welcome to the club. Sometimes it seems like kids want to do anything in the world *except* what we want them to. If we want them to pick up their dirty underwear off of the floor, they'd rather scrub down the hull of a battleship. Anything but do what it is that we want them to. So let's look at some ways that we can increase the chances that they will do what we require and decrease the amount of time we spend yelling and threatening them.

In his book, *Control Theory,* William Glasser said this: people are motivated by five things. He doesn't call them this, but I call them Glasser's Five F's: food & fornicating, fun, friends & family, freedom, and force.

The area that I remember as *Glasser's food & fornicating* is what Glasser calls *survival and reproduction needs.* Let's think first about the food side of the need. In addition to food, that would include air, water, enough clothing to provide adequate warmth, and enough shelter to provide for survival. Since many of our kids come to our homes without having had these things, that's where they often function. That's why they steal food. "Yeah," thinks Shelly, "There is plenty to eat right now, but you never know about tomorrow." She is motivated to steal food because life has taught her that while it may be abundant one day, there may be none the next. After all, the day after the government check came at home, there was always plenty to eat, but as the end of the month approached, there wasn't anything left to eat.

Glasser's reproduction need is referred to as an adult need. However, physical adulthood starts at puberty, and therefore, the sexual urge becomes a need in what we think of as children. Some of our kids come to us having been meeting this need, although probably in psychologically unhealthy ways.

Certainly, in our culture, it is considered wrong for thirteen- and fourteen-year-old kids (as well as older teens) to be sexually active; however, many of our great grandparents may have married as young teens, since they lived in a different historical context than we do. In a world in which the average life expectancy was 45, thirteen was considered an adult. The body was usually capable of reproduction and life was already a third over. In addition, in many countries today, young women marry as young teens and are considered adults at their first menstrual period.

In any event, the point is that our teenagers have a strong sexual need, and many of them have been meeting it before they come to us by having sexual relations. Suddenly, they are living in a structured environment and they find themselves unable to satisfy their sexual need. They will persist in trying to meet this need; however, it is our job to restrict them from engaging in sexual practices for which we believe they are not ready. This leaves them one avenue of fulfilling their sexual need: masturbation.

Along with the survival and reproduction needs, Glasser says that any of the following things can motivate a person depending upon the situation. Since these aren't in any particular order, let's start with what my way of remembering calls *Glasser's friends & family*. Glasser uses the term *the need to belong—to love, share, and cooperate* for this motivator.

When I was a little girl, I overheard someone (I think it was my priest) say that no man is an island. I remember thinking, "How dumb. Of course a man is not an island. A man is a person and an island is a big rock in the water. How could anyone possibly look at a big rock in the water and confuse it with a person?" Gradually I came to understand that by saying no man is an island, my priest (or whoever) meant that we all need people.

We need people, and we need some people more than we need others. As children, we first and foremost need our mother. By the term mother, I am referring to that person that was our primary caretaker when we were a baby. After we have our mother, we need other people in lesser but varying degrees.

As adults, we need a loving mate, or at least a close, loving friend. All adults need friends. These can range from a close, intimate friend (who if you are lucky is your mate) to casual friends that you visit with at morning coffee break or that you bowl with on the league. In addition, many adults want the love of a child, although many adults these days are choosing to remain childless. But regardless of who our family & friends folk are, we all need to feel a sense of belonging and affiliation.

It is the strong drive for belonging and affiliation that leads many kids to join gangs. (Of course, there are other reasons, also, and one of those reasons may be survival.) If you are a child and you don't feel like you are loved at home, if you don't have a sense of belonging and affiliation there, then you are driven to seek it elsewhere. As you enter into your teenage years, you are biologically driven to seek love outside your home. (Thank goodness for that biological drive, else we would all still live with our parents and mate with our immediate family members.) If you are lucky enough to live in an environment in which wholesome friends are available to you, then you develop friendships with those people. If, however, you are unlucky enough to live somewhere that only gang members are available to you as potential friends, then you develop friendships with those people. Either way, you are going to try to meet your affiliation and belonging needs.

What I call *Glasser's fun*, Glasser calls *fun*, too. Let's admit it. We all want to have fun. Different ones of us may find it in different ways. You, for example, may have fun fishing. I would die of boredom trying to fish. (I did try to fish once and that's how I know.) On the other hand, I have fun eating cold asparagus out of a can while watching "Northern Exposure" on TV. You might die of boredom watching "Northern Exposure" and die of being grossed out trying to eat cold asparagus. We each get our kicks in our own ways.

A lot of what kids do that drives us crazy is their attempts at trying to meet their need for fun. Wrestling in the living room floor is fun to teenage boys; the problem is that having boys wrestling on the living room floor drives housemoms nuts. Listening to their music at high volume is fun to teenagers, but it drives housedads nuts. Sneaking out of the house at night to go skinnydipping in the pool not only drives houseparents mad but is also unsafe without appropriate supervision; however, our kids persist in trying to do it because it is fun, and one of humankind's basic drives is the drive to have fun.

The last one, I call *Glasser's force*. He calls it the need for *power*. None of us likes to feel like we are powerless. Says Glasser: "This need to get others to obey us, and the esteem that accompanies it, drives all of us. Even the most humble compete with other self-effacers for humility" (p. 10).

Our kids, then, compete with each other to be the best athlete, the coolest dude, the hottest chick, the baddest ass, or the biggest stud. They also challenge us for power. New houseparents get challenged for power the worst; since they haven't established their place in the herd, they have to prove to the kids that they are alpha wolves in the pack.

The term *alpha wolf* refers to being the head wolf. Alpha, the first letter of the Greek alphabet, refers to being first. Wolves in the second line of power in the pecking order in the pack are called *beta wolves,* since beta is the second letter in the Greek alphabet. Omega is the last letter, so the term *omega wolf* refers to those who are at the bottom of the pecking order.

This notion of pecking order is extremely important when living and working with other people's kids. It would be worthwhile to have a better understanding of this phenomenon.

In 1922, a young Norwegian scientist, T. Schjelderup-Ebbe, reported to the scientific community that he had been studying social dominance in chickens. He called this the pecking order. Schjelderup-Ebbe found that in every flock of chickens there was a top chicken. He called this chicken the alpha chicken, so he was the first person to use the term alpha in this way, and it was therefore to him that we owe the term alpha wolf. He explained that the alpha chicken could peck every other bird in the flock, but none could peck her back. They knew better than to even try.

Followed in dominance by the alpha chicken was the beta chicken. She could peck any chicken under her in dominance and they could not peck her back, and so on. At the bottom of the pecking order was the poor, pitiful, old omega chicken. Life was hardly worth living for this old girl. Everyone could peck her and she couldn't peck anyone back.

In order to see whether pecking orders existed in other species of birds, Schjelderup-Ebbe studied sparrows, pheasants, ducks, geese, cockatoos, parrots, and canaries. Sure enough, they all had a pecking order.

In 1964, C. R. Carpenter decided to find out whether the pecking order existed among primates. He studied a variety of monkeys and apes and found that primates do have pecking order. However, in contrast to the birds, the pecking order among primates was somewhat more subtle.

Whereas the pecking order was firmly established among birds, rank consisted of *tendencies* for one monkey to precede the next in social order in the primate world.

Carpenter also found that the severity with which the pecking order was maintained varied among species. For example, among Rhesus monkeys, rank was pulled quickly and severely. A higher rank Rhesus would whop a lower rank one in a minute if the lower challenged the higher one for a piece of fruit. Carpenter called this a *high dominance gradient.* In contrast, a higher ranking Arboreal Howler monkey would rarely pull rank on a lower ranking one. He might let the lower ranking monkey have the mango in question and pick another one for himself. Carpenter called this *low dominance gradient.*

Among human kids, athletic prowess and good looks are the primary characteristics that place a person in the pecking order. Everyone knows that the good-looking high school quarterback has the most prestige in the school and the funny-looking little guy who works in the cafeteria has the least. In the same way, everyone knows that the head cheerleader, whose face and body are both beautiful, has much more social power than the girl who sits in the back of math class trying to hide her overweight body and acne.

So all of us are engaged in the struggle to have power, although we may seek it in different arenas. For example, while my neighbor may seek power by being the best tennis player in the country club, I seek power by trying to influence the people who read my books. My neighbor is seeking power in a constructive way, and since I am trying to use my power need to make people live more satisfying lives, so am I. Seeking power isn't necessarily a bad thing, but it certainly can be. Many of our kids won't be mature enough to seek power in positive ways; many of them will have seen adults only seek power in negative ways, such as by physically abusing others. Therefore, many of our kids will physically abuse each other as they try to meet their power needs.

The need for power may directly conflict with the need for belonging, love, and cooperation. Most of our kids come to us feeling powerless; some social agency has taken over their already powerless lives and made them come live with us. So while they especially need to feel loved and a part of our family, they also especially need to feel powerful.

Karen may desperately need to feel like she is part of our foster family, but her need for power may result in her behaving in ways that make us not want her in our family. She talks back to us in order to express her need for power, so we are inclined to express our need for power by isolating her in her room. Since she is hungry for love and fellowship also, she has met her power need at the expense of her love need. It is a precariously balanced scale.

Gabe was a teenage boy who came to us feeling powerless and unloved. While he wanted to be loved and thereby meet his belonging need, he also was wild to have his power need met. In order to meet his power need, he abused the younger kids by hitting them, kicking them, grabbing their testicles, and threatening them. This made us need to express our power need over him and thereby protect the younger children. He was never able to find a balanced way to meet both needs, and we finally had to send him away in order to protect the younger kids.

The last motivator in Glasser's theory is *freedom*. People lay down their lives for freedom. Our very country was founded on this principle. It's no wonder that the desire for freedom is one of the basic motivators for human beings. In many group homes and institutions there isn't much freedom for kids. Their whole lives are regulated. We need to find ways to give kids some feeling of freedom to make choices for themselves. By freedom, I'm not talking about license. Responsibility is a partner of freedom. What I am talking about is the right to make responsible choices.

So how can a houseparent use each of these things to motivate kids? Before I discuss ways that we can use these needs to motivate kids, I need to explain that Glasser says that all of our behavior is designed to help us control things in our lives in order to meet our needs. For example, when I write, I am trying to control my world so that I might meet my survival and power needs in ways that I choose. Since writing is part of my income, it helps me buy food and therefore meets my survival needs. Since it fulfills my need for power in the attempt to influence the thinking of my readers, it meets my power need.

So how can we help kids control their worlds to meet their needs in ways that will be mutually beneficial for them and us both? We're going to discuss that in a moment, but before we do, we need to talk about *intrinsic vs. extrinsic motivation.*

Intrinsic motivation is doing something because you want to do it. You might say that you feel driven to do it. Glasser would say that you are driven to do it because it meets your survival & reproduction needs or your needs for belonging, fun, freedom, or power. Intrinsic motivation means a motivation that comes from inside of you.

In contrast, some researchers say that extrinsic motivation is motivation that arises from outside of you. These researchers say that instead of doing something because you feel driven to do it, you do that thing because of external influences. These external motivators include rewards, bribes, threats, deadlines, being evaluated by others, or being supervised by others. Extrinsic motivation is a poor excuse for doing something, from a kid's point of view.

Glasser would agree with the kid. In fact, Glasser would say that there is no such thing as extrinsic motivation. Extrinsic motivation simply does not exist. People don't do things for extrinsic motivation. They do things that get their F-needs met. It may appear that people are reacting to extrinsic motivators, but when offered an extrinsic motivator, they ask, "Does this help me meet my needs?" If the offered carrot is need-satisfying, a kid takes a bite. If the offered carrot isn't need-satisfying, the kid goes on his merry way.

As houseparents, we try to control kids by reward and punishment. We have a hard time understanding why sometimes a reward or punishment works with a kid, and at other times, the same reward or punishment doesn't work with that kid. Whether or not the reward or punishment is effective at a given time lies in the kid's answer to this question: Will this satisfy my needs?

Take for example, Emerson's niece, Melissa. When Melissa was two years old, she went to visit her grandma. Melissa's mom gave strict instructions that Melissa should not be allowed to climb the stairs. Aunt Nini was tending Melissa when Melissa decided that she was going to climb the stairs.

"If you climb those stairs, I'm going to spank you," said Aunt Nini.

Melissa looked at Aunt Nini and then back at the stairs. She sighed and then said, "Well, I think that I'm just going to climb those stairs anyway." And up she went.

Melissa climbed the stairs because it satisfied her need for fun, freedom, or power, and the threat of a spanking didn't slow her down.

Like Melissa, I became a houseparent because I was internally motivated to do it. It satisfied my needs of family & friends, fun, force, and freedom. I didn't do it for the money; in fact, I took a drastic pay cut and reduction in prestige in order to do it. I did it for intrinsic motivation.

But as time went on, like most houseparents, I grew tired. I no longer was able to meet my survival needs, because the constant stressors of being a houseparent brought me ill health which was manifested in a variety of ways: endometriosis, weight gain, and depression. I had to leave houseparenting after eighteen months in order to meet my basic survival needs again. It wouldn't have mattered if they had offered me a million dollars a year to stay on.

So intrinsic motivation is doing something because it meets one of our Glasserian F-needs, and external motivation is doing something for any reason outside of meeting our F-needs: to secure some type of a reward or to avoid a threat. Extrinsic motivation is a type of external constraint. Other external constraints include: meeting deadlines imposed by others, being evaluated by others, or being supervised by others. "Whoa!" you might be thinking. "Rewards are not constraints!"

Oh, yes they are. The guy who rewards you is the one who is in charge. He is the Big Boss who gives orders and sets rules; he rewards you to keep you in line. Think about it.

So when April makes her bed because you put a contingency on it (If you make your bed, then you can play), you're placing external constraints on her.

Now that you understand the difference between intrinsic and extrinsic motivation (which is a form of external constraint), let's continue.

Okay, one of the big problems with many children's homes (and especially with public schools) is that they are based on extrinsic constraint. The big person tells the little person what he has to do (and by when), and then the big person oversees the activity, bribing or threatening to get it done, and then evaluates and rewards or punishes the little person. But external constraints, including material rewards, reduce performance, creativity, and task interest, and encourage passive behavior! This is called the *undermining effect.*

Take for example, the child who wants to come into the kitchen and help cook. Let's call him Brad. When Brad asks if he can help you make cookies, then he is being motivated by an internal force. But if you reward him for helping you, then you have imposed external constraints, and his future interest in making cookies will be reduced. Extrinsic motivation undermines intrinsic motivation. It is important to note that this is true for people of all ages, and that it is especially true for young children.

A related result of extrinsic rewards is the *minimax strategy.* The minimax strategy is using the least amount of effort necessary in order to obtain the maximum amount of reward. We've all dealt with kids who use the minimax strategy. What surprised me when I became a college professor is that so many adults use the minimax strategy also. The first assignment that I received from my adult students broke my heart. Many of the students had exerted only a small amount of effort, "But these are adults!" I thought. "Adults know better!" Ah, yes. They *know* better, but they don't *do* better. They've been well trained by a school system that uses external constraints to get by with as little effort as possible, so they become adults who do as little as they possibly can to get by.

That brings us to a related issue: if outside constraints reduce performance, how do we get a kid to do things that have to be done if the kid isn't internally motivated to do it by one of Glasser's needs?

Let's skip talking about using kids' survival needs, because it's immoral for us to mess around with a kid's survival needs to get him to do something that we want him to do. We're not going to withhold food from Tommy in order to get him to obey us, nor are we going to make him go outside in the cold without his coat so that he'll be stimulated to do his chores. In addition, we're certainly not going to reward him by telling him that he can have sex with his girlfriend if he gets his chores done, so I don't see using Tommy's drive to meet his survival needs as a useful tool for us as houseparents. So we'll move directly on to the need to belong, or to have friends & family.

When I was a kid, I would frustrate my mom by not cleaning my room like she wanted me to. But I loved to go over to a friend's house and help her clean her room. My friends were in the same situation. They drove their moms crazy by not cleaning their rooms, but they loved to come over and help me clean mine. Now, put on your Sherlock Holmes hat and draw a conclusion here: let kids work together to clean their rooms! "Okay, Billy and Barry," you say. "Your rooms have to get clean. You can each work on your own room, or you can work together on one room and then on the other."

I'm not saying that you won't go in thirty minutes later and find Billy and Barry lying on the floor playing with their Hot Wheels cars. You may well do just that. But on the other hand, the same thing would probably happen if each boy were working alone. At least this way, the chore will be viewed as less drudgery and the boys will begin to ever so slowly develop more positive attitudes about doing work. In short, the chore will become more fun and therefore meet two of Glasser's needs (belonging and fun) instead of none.

This leads us to the next area, which is fun. Let me develop the story of my girlfriends and me cleaning our rooms. When my friends Paula or

Sharli would come over and help me clean my room, we had a special game we played. My favorite auntie had given me a set of Ozark dolls whose heads were made of walnuts. Each doll had a painted face and fake hair. Each was painstakingly dressed clear down to her bloomers. Each doll had her official name pinned to her dress.

My favorite doll was the first one that my aunt ever gave me, and her name was Aunt Poodie. (The doll's name, that is, not my aunt's name. My aunt's name was Doris.) Aunt Poodie had a stern face and a ferocious countenance. Although there was a granny doll in the collection, it was Aunt Poodie that was the unquestioned matriarch of the clan.

Now, when Paula or Sharli would come over, we would set all the dolls on my dresser, arranged like General Patton and his troops, and you can guess who was the general of this outfit. Then we pretended like my room was a mansion owned by Aunt Poodie and inhabited by her and the rest of the Walnuthead family. We girls were the maids, of course, and our job was to clean the room to Aunt Poodie's approval. So we giggled and laughed as we worked and asked Aunt Poodie's direction about what should be done and in what order, and we made housecleaning fun. In this way, I incorporated two of my needs into the work: family & friends and fun.

I'm not saying that you have to buy fierce-looking dolls to motivate your younger kids to clean their rooms. What I am saying is that when you team kids together, they're more likely to make the chore into a game, and there are a gazillion ways of doing that.

One way is by using a timer and suggesting that the kids play beat-the-clock. I still sometimes do that, but I use "number of songs" as the timer. I'll put on a favorite tape of energetic music and see if I can finish cleaning the kitchen before a given number of songs is finished. Even in middle age, housework is more enjoyable if you can find a game aspect to it.

When I taught first grade, the kids and I sometimes played "Army" when it was time to clean up the room at the end of the day. I was the general, a couple of kids would be appointed as sergeant, and everyone else was a private. First we would snap to attention and I would salute to the troops, who would salute back. Then we would march around the room a time or two. Then I would turn on a John Phillips Sousa march, and each soldier would frantically start cleaning whatever she could see that needed cleaning, while the sergeant ran around and pointed out things that were overlooked. We tried to finish the job before the end of the song. Then we all ran to our seats, snapped back to attention and I, as the general, inspected the room and congratulated the troops. It was a hoot.

We can help kids meet their power needs while doing their chores in a variety of ways. One way that we can help kids meet their power needs is by participatory decision making. When we let kids decide select which chores from a list that they will do, we are using participatory decision making. Tommy is controlling his world in a way which meets his power need when he selects chores to do, rather than being told which chores he has to do.

When we give kids recognition for doing a good job on their chores, we are helping them meet their power needs by praising them for doing what needs to be done in the cottage. You probably have one kid in the cottage who is always volunteering to help you. This kid is trying to meet his power need through gaining your recognition. The problem inherent in this scenario is that Tommy may be meeting his power needs through gaining your approval, while he is concurrently failing to meet his belonging needs, since the other guys call him a brownnoser for trying to please you.

In the same way that participatory decision making helps kids meet their power needs, participatory decision making also helps kids meet their need for freedom. Although Tommy probably prefers to do no chores at all, having the freedom to choose what chores he will do is a heckova lot better than being told what chores he has to do.

Participatory decision making helps kids meet their needs for power, freedom, and also belonging. You can find ways other than the assignment of chores to give kids chances to engage in participatory decision making. Do your kids get to vote on where they go on recreation nights? Do they get to vote on what they want for Sunday dinner? For bedtime snacks? We adults make lots of decisions for kids that the kids ought to be making for themselves. After all, that kind of decision making helps our kids meet their power and freedom needs in constructive ways, and if they can't meet those needs in constructive ways, they are going to meet them in destructive ways.

We are going to behave in ways that meet our needs. If those needs are thwarted, we feel like our life is out of control. If we feel like our lives are out of control, we are genetically programmed to feel angry. Feeling angry stimulates us to try and change our situation. However, we may swallow that anger and stop trying to meet our needs. We then feel depressed and helpless. That feeling of helplessness comes from believing that we can't change the present situation in order to meet our needs. Helplessness can become *learned helplessness.* Learned helplessness is believing that we can't change a situation, so we don't even try.

Learned helplessness was discovered by a fellow named Martin Seligman. Seligman put dogs in a cage in which half the floor was wired for electric shock and half was not. The dogs quickly learned that if they were standing on the electrified half of the floor and the electricity came on, they could escape the shock by jumping to the other side of the cage.

Then, however, Seligman wired both sides of the floor. Now, when the dog was on the side that he thought was safe, he would still be shocked. Now, he could not escape pain. Regardless of where he stood he was shocked.

Finally, the researchers unwired the half of the cage that had originally been the safe side. It was now safe once again. But now, the dog wouldn't jump to the safe side when he was shocked on the "hot" side. He didn't realize that he could stop the shock by going back to the safe side, so he just sat on the electrified side and quivered. He had given up. He had learned that he had no control over the shock, so he accepted it rather than trying to get away from it.

Once the dog had learned helplessness, Seligman had to drag him to the safe side over and over and over before he had relearned that he could escape the shock by going to the other side of the cage.

When Darrin experiences failure after failure, he learns that whether he fails or succeeds in not under his control, that nothing that he does matters. He will attribute his failure to his own internal and unchangeable inability to be smart. A researcher by the name of Weiner explains it this way: There are two variables involved here. The first variable is this: Is the situation within my power to control (internal) or outside of my power to control (external)? The second variable is this: Is this a constant state of affairs (stable) or a changeable one (unstable)?

Darrin thinks "I'm stupid," after he fails a test. "I fail because I'm dumb. Because I'm dumb, nothing that I can do will make a difference. I will always fail." He thinks that his failure is due to something internal and stable: his IQ. If Darrin does pass the test, he attributes his success to something outside of him: luck or ease of task. If he believes that it is external and stable, he believes that his success is due to ease of the task: "The test was too easy." If he believes that his success was due to factors that are external and unstable, then he believes that his success was due to luck: "I succeeded, because I was lucky."

Darrin doesn't understand that his success or failure might be due to something internal and unstable: effort. If he did understand that, then he would think, "I failed. But I failed because I didn't put enough effort into it. I should have studied more. Next time I will." Or if he had succeeded, he would think, "I passed because I studied hard."

If Darrin gets beat up because he didn't clean his room good enough to please his parents, then the same thing happens; he will attribute his failure to internal, stable factors: "I'm dumb; nothing I can do will change that." He won't attribute it to internal, unstable factors (effort), to external, stable factors (Mom and Dad are unreasonable), or to external, unstable factors: (Mom and Dad had a bad day.)

The key to working with kids who have learned helplessness is helping them change their beliefs about the source of their failure. If Darrin's failure to meet your approval in cleaning his room was due to his lack of effort, then explain that to him. Make certain that he understands that it is not because he is too dumb to know how to do it, but that because it requires more effort than he gave and that he can change that.

If it sounds ridiculous to you that a child could think that he didn't pass room inspection because he's too dumb, think again. If you were Darrin and raised in a home in which nothing you did could please your parents regardless of how hard you tried, then you, too, would soon come to believe that it was because you were too stupid to get it right. Remember that that is where many of our kids have come from.

The key here is to change kids' beliefs that failure is going to be the result of whatever they do, so they might as well not even try. Help them learn that *effort* changes things. Tell them that over and over. But also create situations in which they prove it to themselves and then tell them what they've proven. In the Jaime Escalante movie, the true story of the math teacher who was so successful teaching calculus to his inner-city Hispanic students, Jaime keeps saying to the kids, "*Ganas!* You gotta have *ganas!*" and "You can do it! You can do it!" *Ganas* means *desire,* and what Jaime means is, "You gotta want it and work for it!"

A word of warning here, though. If the child's reason for failure *is* due to lack of ability, then we don't want to teach him that he just didn't try hard enough. If a child isn't reasonably bright, he is never going to understand algebra, regardless of how hard he tries. We don't want to go on telling him, "You could do it if you would just apply yourself." Get real. He can't do it any more than I could swim the English Channel. He just doesn't have the ability. Under these circumstances, we need to change the requirements of the task so that he has a reasonable chance of success. The external conditions need to be changed and we have to be the ones to change those conditions.

Now that we're talking about effort making things change, we need to think about the notion of challenge, which requires effort, as opposed to guaranteed success, which does not.

Many houseparents (and teachers) have been so well taught the saying, "Nothing breeds success like success," that they believe that they must guarantee success for their children in every endeavor. Hogwash. Guaranteed success *reduces* performance. It is *moderate risk of failure and the achievement of moderate success* that increases not only performance but persistence, pride, maximum satisfaction, self-knowledge, and perceived competence. Let me explain.

An important principle of motivation is this: tasks that we have a moderate chance of succeeding at (50%) bring us the most intrinsic rewards; in fact, moderate probability of success is said to be an essential ingredient in intrinsic motivation. I think this may be because of the fun factor. If we know without a doubt that we can succeed at something, it isn't fun any more. Likewise, if we know that we cannot possibly succeed, then it isn't fun either. Only when we think that we have a moderate chance of succeeding at a task is it fun for us. For example, is it fun to go bowling with a guy you know can't beat you? No. Is it fun to go bowling with a guy you know that you can't beat? No. It is only fun to go bowling with someone with whom you are well matched, because then your chance of success is about 50%.

If you know that you will always beat him, then your win is external and stable (winning is too easy) and internal and stable (you have more ability than he does). If you know that you can never beat him, then your win is still internal and stable: he has more ability than you do. But if you are evenly matched in ability (internal and stable), then your win is based on effort, which is internal and unstable. (And some darn good luck.)

What about this? What about if your chance for success is about 20%? The odds are stacked against you, but you just might win. How do you feel when you don't have a fighting chance? Research shows us that you will then attribute a win to an external, unstable force: luck. It's not near as fun to win because you were lucky as it is to win because you tried harder.

Succeeding at a challenging task (50% odds of success) makes us feel proud, competent, determined, persistent, and in personal control. It's great!

Moderate risk taking refers to carefully choosing a challenging task which you know that you might fail but at which, with effort, you might succeed. This combination: personal control in selecting the task, moderate success, and finding out how you did, that holds the attention, and creates energy, in people who become obsessed with an activity.

The following conditions are conducive to risk taking: First, the probability of success is clear. (About half the time I beat him when we bowl, and about half the time he beats me. We're evenly matched.)

Second, external constraints are minimized. (We're doing this just for the fun of it. No one is paying us for it, and no one is forcing us to do it.)

Third, there is a variable payoff. What this means is that the value of success increases as risk increases, in contrast to a fixed payoff. (If I give him a five-pin handicap, it would be a real hoot to beat him then! Because then there would be greater risk of my failure! So if I won, he'd really have to take a ribbing! Worse than if we played even odds!)

Fourth, the benefits of risk taking can be anticipated. (Boy, it will be a ball if I can beat him and rub his nose in it!)

Let's translate that into cottage chores.

The house has to be cleaned. There are ten kids in the house, ranging from ten to fifteen years of age. You make up the list of chores, assigning a number value to each, such as: vacuum living room, 20 pts.; dust living room, 5 pts.; take out trash, 5 pts., and so on. The total number of points a team of two kids can earn in a twenty-minute dash determines the winners. Each team chooses three chores, and the winning team is the one that successfully completes the chores which total the most number of points in the allotted time. Various numbers of points earn rewards with various values. For example, 60 points might mean staying up late, whereas 30 points means a lesser reward, such as getting to choose the cottage's bedtime snack.

The difference between this and telling the kids, "If you do your chores, then you can stay up late," is that because in the game format, risk was involved, external constraints were minimized, there was a variable payoff, and the benefits of the risk were anticipated, so it became fun and therefore an intrinsic motivator. Viola! Just like magic!

Margaret Clifford, a motivation researcher at the University of Iowa, sums up how to use risk taking to get the most out of kids:
1. Have plenty of opportunities to risk take.
2. Provide explicit information about probability of success.
3. Keep a relaxed and non-threatening environment.
4. Have payoffs vary with task difficulty.
5. Keep the chores relatively free of external constraints.
6. Give immediate feedback about level of success and errors.

The feedback is essential in the risk taking. If we think that we always succeed, then our success becomes meaningless. We have to know when we did not succeed and why. Only then can we improve our performance.

In this chapter, we have talked about how to motivate children in our cottages. We learned about Glasser's theory of internal motivation, which I call Glasser's Five F's: food & fornication, family & friends, fun, force, and freedom. We also learned that success or failure is based upon internal or external, and stable or unstable conditions. We learned that if we attribute our failure to the internal, stable condition of ability, then we develop learned helplessness. We learned that as houseparents, we can help a child overcome learned helplessness by teaching him to attribute his failure or success to the internal, unstable condition of effort.

We have also learned about external constraints and that those constraints, including rewards, decrease motivation and actually reduce performance. However, because we learned about moderate success probability and moderate risk taking, we learned how we can turn chores into fun, and thereby use an internal motivator to get our kids to do their chores.

In the next chapter, we are going to talk about how learning takes place, not only so that you can better understand the process of teaching your kids their daily living skills, but also so that you won't feel intimidated by trying to help them with their homework.

Chapter 10

HOW TO TEACH KIDS

In the last chapter, we talked about ways to motivate kids to do what you want them to. In this chapter, we're going to discuss how to teach kids, whether you are trying to teach them how to do their independent living skills, or whether you are trying to help teach them how to do their homework.

In the last sentence, you may have thought that it was strange that I used the phrase *teach them how to do their homework* instead of *tutor them on their homework*. I used the word teach instead of tutor because the activity is the same. We tend to think of tutoring as a second class activity as opposed to teaching. That is not the case. Teaching is teaching and we should honor that.

While most every houseparent feels competent to help kids learn their independent living skills (caring for their clothing, cleaning house, using good manners, getting along with their peers, accepting direction from authority, etc.), most houseparents don't consider that teaching. But it *is* teaching.

In contrast to teaching those independent living skills, most houseparents don't feel competent to help teach kids their homework. That's where houseparents are fooling themselves. With the exception of some of the higher math and science courses, any houseparent who graduated from high school and who can read, can help teach kids their homework.

When I was a housemom, our children's home hired college kids to come in for two hours every afternoon to teach the kids their homework. I would have loved to have had the extra money that went to the college kids, but that wasn't an option. Somehow, the children's home had the notion that houseparents couldn't teach kids their homework. Maybe the home had started that at the houseparents' request years ago. I don't know. But the fact remains that money was going to the college kids when we houseparents could have used it.

Lest you should think, "But you wouldn't have had time with fixing dinner and all," that wasn't the case. We had a cafeteria on the ranch and, except for Sunday nights, everyone ate dinner in the cafeteria. Then the boys were in charge of cleaning the cafeteria and kitchen afterward under the supervision of the dads. So trying to get dinner ready during study time wasn't an issue.

"But I couldn't help kids with their homework! I don't know the first thing about teaching!" you may be thinking. Let me set you straight. You know a whole lot about teaching. For example, if you have ever raised a child from birth (your own child or someone else's), can it speak English? If so, then who do you think taught it to? Can it dress itself? Who do you think taught it to? Can it cross the street without getting whacked by a passing car? Who do you think taught it to? Parents were teaching their children for thousands of years before anyone was ever given the title of teacher.

The same skills that you used in teaching your baby how to speak, dress, and cross the streets are the same skills that you use to teach your children other things, including their homework. So follow me and learn how much that you already know.

In order to talk about how teaching and learning take place, we are going to talk about a Russian guy named Lev Vygotsky. (It is pronounced just like it looks.)

Vygotsky was a young Russian social psychologist at the time of the Russian Revolution in 1917. He was doing lots of research and publishing at that time, and the scientific community was beginning to sit up and take notice. Here was one bright guy.

About that time, Vygotsky fell in love with the niece of one of the higher ups in the new Communist regime, so Vygotsky began being known among the powerful people at the top. It wasn't long before the regime needed someone to come up with a theory of teaching and learning around which the re-education camps could be organized, so guess who got the job.

Now that what the Communists called *re-education camps,* you and I know were concentration camps, where unspeakable horrors took place. We can rest assured that the people who committed those crimes against humanity lie rotting in hell, but what we are trying to talk about here is how the camps were supposed to work in theory, not how they worked in reality.

So Vygotsky was supposed to develop a theory of teaching and learning that was in tune with Marxist principles. Since Marx said that work is good and that through working, people could be reeducated, Vygotsky had to center his theory around work, which wasn't hard to do.

It was Vygotsky's theory then, which was originally developed to organize the re-education camps' learning programs, that we are going to talk about here. Don't hold its beginnings against poor old Vygotsky. The theory is wonderfully humane, regardless of its shady origin.

Vygotsky's theory of teaching and learning is called the *Socially Mediated Apprenticeship Theory*. If you forget the rest of the title, just remember the word apprenticeship, because if you can remember that much, you'll remember the general idea: a master guiding an apprentice through a task.

> Vygotsky said that *teaching* is simply *assisting performance*. He said that *learning* is simply *performing with assistance*.

When you have a new kid in your cottage and you help him make his bed the first few times so that he sees how you want it done, you are teaching him. You are assisting his performance in making the bed, and he is performing with assistance. That's teaching and learning.

If he asks you to help him with his subtraction and you help him work a problem, you are assisting his performance and he is performing with assistance. That's teaching and learning.

"So," you may say, "That's just helping. Is all helping teaching?"

No. It depends. If you are assisting someone in performing something that he is *capable of learning*, then you are teaching him. But if you are assisting someone to do something that he is *not* capable of learning, then you are not teaching him. For example, if I dress the baby and he is not capable of learning to dress himself yet, then I am not teaching him. I am just dressing him. But if he has reached the point where he can begin learning how to dress himself, then I am teaching him while I am dressing him. Whether or not you are teaching depends on whether or not the student has the capacity to learn what you are assisting him to do.

In the same way that you are not teaching Dillon to dress himself if he doesn't have the capacity to learn to dress himself, you are not teaching him to dress himself if he can *already* dress himself. Then you are just getting in his way. A good example of this is a backseat driver. You know how to drive, but the backseat driver keeps trying to assist your performance. He says, "Speed up to get around that car! Turn on your turn signal! Slow down for that stop sign ahead!" He annoys the dickens out of you, because he is trying to assist your performance in an activity which you can already perform. He can't teach you what you already know how to do.

So the psychological space in which we learn things exists between the place where we have the capacity to learn some new thing, and the place where we have already developed our capacity to learn that thing. Vygotsky calls that place the Zone of Proximal Development (ZPD).

The word proximal means close to, so the Zone of Proximal Development is the area close to the person's development.

The first stage of learning in the ZPD is having assistance provided by others. This is the place in which you teach Dillon to dress himself. The second stage in the ZPD is the place where Dillon assists himself. He hasn't yet learned to automatically dress himself without thinking about it, but he doesn't need you helping him anymore. Now he assists himself by talking himself through each step.

This is why we talk to ourselves. We are assisting our own performance! For example, when I first move into a new town, I have to ask people how to get places, so they are assisting me. As time goes on, I don't have to ask people, but until I can put my mind in automatic pilot and drive where I want to go without thinking about how to get there, I have to assist myself.

"Okay, here at the light I go three blocks east. . . . There's the hardware store. That means that I want to turn at the next corner" I say to myself, and in this way I am assisting my own performance. After a while, I will be able to get into my car and drive wherever I want to go without thinking about how to get there.

Another example is how we talk to ourselves when we are working through a problem with our spouse. Say you have a fight with your wife. You walk around talking to yourself about it. What you are doing is trying to assist yourself in understanding the fight and figuring out how to resolve it. "She said that I don't listen to her. What did she mean by that? I always listen to her! What am I doing that makes her think that? Is it because I don't act interested? I wonder what would happen if I started nodding my head when she talks?"

You are talking to yourself because you don't have a ready plan to solve the problem and you need some assistance. You don't need so much assistance that you need to go to someone else to help you (a friend or counselor), but you do need some assistance, so you are assisting yourself.

And all this time, you thought that you were a little crazy when you talked to yourself! Now you know that you were just assisting your own performance!

Once Dillon no longer needs to talk himself through dressing himself, or I no longer have to talk myself through the route when driving to work, then we have fossilized the skill. Other learning theories call this internalization or automatization, but Vygotsky calls it *fossilization* and I like that. When something is a fossil, it is set in stone and there for good, isn't it? So the word fossilization works well for me, because it reminds me how permanent learning is.

Fossilization is where Dillon's or my skill stays from then on, unless Dillon or I defossilize the skill.

Defossilization occurs when we lose our knowledge of how to do a skill for some reason. Probably the most common cause of defossilization is a stroke. But forgetting how to do something out of disuse is also defossilization. For example, if you haven't ridden a bicycle in years, you might have defossilized that skill.

When you have defossilized a skill and need it back, say for example that you have had a stroke and forgotten how to feed yourself, then you go back to an earlier stage. In the case of rehabilitation centers for stroke victims, the therapists teach you to feed yourself all over again.

Or maybe you don't need them to teach you. Maybe you just need to talk yourself through the steps. "Okay, this thing is a spoon and I use it for the soup. I dip it in . . . Oops, it all fell out. . . . I hold it this way to keep from spilling it . . . " and so on.

Typically, when we defossilize from disuse, we return to Stage 2 and just reteach ourselves; we seldom have to have someone else teach us all over again.

One example of defossilization may occur in group homes when the kids have gone home to their families for vacation. Dillon may return remembering nothing that he knew when he left. It may be due to disuse, or it may be due to being emotionally upset, but either way, he may have defossilized and you may have to help reteach him the skills that he lost.

The next point that I want to make is that Vygotsky says that within every interaction between teacher and student (or master and apprentice) the student learns not only the knowledges and the behaviors that you teach him (we hold our fork this way [a behavior] because it is not polite to hold it like that [a knowledge]) but also emotions. For example, by the way that you interact with Dillon when you help him dress himself, you teach him that he should be proud that he can dress himself. When you teach Sharon to operate the vacuum cleaner, you either teach her that it feels good to contribute to the family by doing chores, or that it is a drag.

While I could give you a number of examples from your house, I want to use an example that is personally important to me at this stage of my life.

One of the courses I teach is research for students working on a master's degree in education or counseling. Most students fear taking research, because it is the most difficult course in a master's program. One of my goals, however, is to make my students excited about doing research, so I carefully plan to make statements while I work with them that are designed to teach them the emotions that I want them to have about research.

As we work, I'll stop and say, "Isn't this a blast! I love doing research!" Or I might say, "What a hoot! I'd rather do this than eat ice cream!" At first, my students look at me like I'm crazy, but by the end of the course, they start telling me how much they love doing research and how much fun it is. What they are doing is learning the appropriate emotions about doing research as they are learning the behaviors and knowledges that I want them to have.

What that means is that as adults teaching children, we have an enormous moral responsibility to teach the proper emotions (also read morals here) that we want our student to have about various skills. Whether we realize it or not, we are teaching emotions. Are we teaching the emotions that we should? For example, as I teach a boy to clean the kitchen, am I teaching him to be proud of his contribution to the family, or am I making him do it as a punishment and teaching him that work is bad by saying such things as, "Well, you broke the rules and now you have to take the punishment of cleaning the kitchen." (I am inclined to think that work is a lousy choice of punishment, because people learn to hate work if they have been taught that it is punishment. People should be taught that work is a joy.)

If I am helping Samantha with her homework, I can either look interested and say, "Isn't this neat! It's so much fun to read this history and learn about it!" and thereby teach her positive emotions about studying, or I can say, "This is so boring," or demonstrate by my subtle behaviors that I think it's boring, and therefore teach Samantha negative emotions about studying.

Let's review for a minute before we go on.

Teaching is assisting performance.

Learning is performing with assistance.

Learning takes place in the Zone of Proximal Development, or ZPD.

The ZPD begins when a learner has the capacity to learn something and ends when he has learned that thing.

Stage 1 is performance assisted by others.

Trying to assist someone who doesn't need anymore assistance from us just aggravates them, such as a backseat driver does.

Stage 2 is performance assisted by self.

A person talks to herself when she is assisting her own performance in Stage 2.

When someone no longer needs any assistance in performing a task, she has fossilized the skill.

A skill remains fossilized unless something such as a stroke or disuse defossilizes it.

When a skill is defossilized, the person must go back to an earlier stage of learning.

In every interaction with the teacher, a student learns not only the knowledges and behaviors of the skill, but also the emotions that go along with it.

Your next logical question is, "How do I assist someone?"

That's easy. A researcher by the name of Jerome Bruner described to us the notion of *scaffolding*. Bruner said that we must keep the goal the same for a student as we would for a master and then give the student whatever amount of help she needed in meeting that goal. Providing the amount of assistance a student needs in reaching a goal is what Bruner called scaffolding.

Think of scaffolding like this. Samantha wants to reach an apple in the tree. She isn't tall enough. You build a scaffold just exactly tall enough to allow her to reach the apple.

As she grows taller, she doesn't need the scaffold as high, so you lower it. You always keep the scaffold just exactly tall enough for her to reach the apple, gradually lowering the scaffold as she grows taller. When she is finally tall enough to reach the apple by standing on the ground, you fold up your scaffold and walk away.

You have allowed her to do what she can do, and you have done the rest to assure that she could reach the apple. That is a good metaphor for teaching. You give Samantha just enough assistance to allow her to successfully complete the task, gradually reducing your assistance as her ability grows.

Let's say the task is to bake a chocolate cake. Samantha can read the recipe out loud, but she doesn't know how to measure the flour. Have her do whatever she can do, and you assist her to do the rest. If you have to measure the flour and she can't help at all in measuring the flour, then so be it. Don't do any more than she needs you to do, but don't do any less, either. Do what you have to do for a good cake to be made.

Gradually, as Samantha can do more and more, you do less and less, just as you would lower the scaffold.

Now that you know that teaching is assisting performance, there are a million ways that performance can be assisted. However, educational researchers say that types of assistance can generally be broken down into the following. These levels of assistance go from the most intensive level of assistance to no assistance at all:

1. physical guidance
2. modeling
3. direct verbal
4. indirect verbal
5. gesturing
6. natural cue (no assistance)

In the case of physical guidance, you physically take Samantha's hand, fold it around the measuring cup handle, hold her wrist as you dip it in the flour, and so on. You probably won't often have to resort to physical guidance, unless you work with kids with moderate to severe disabilities. However, one time when you may have to use physical guidance is when a child is having a serious acting-out episode. You may have to say, "Jennifer, I know that you are angry, but I will not allow you to keep banging your head against the wall. Can you stop on your own, or do you need me to help you stop? If you cannot stop on your own, then I will physically hold you so that you cannot bang your head." You are assisting her in her performance of stopping her acting out. You are teaching her to stop the behavior.

Let me add that rich people get physical guidance from their golf or tennis coach when the coach stands behind them at the golf tee and, wrapping his hands around theirs on the club, physically guides them through the swing. So if you get a job as a golf or tennis coach, you will know what to call what you are doing: physical guidance.

Less intensive than physical guidance is modelling. In modelling, you show the child how to do something and then let her try it. You would dip the measuring cup into the flour, while Samantha watched. You are teaching her!

Less intensive still is direct verbal assistance. This is probably the most frequently used level of assistance. Direct verbal assistance is simply telling someone something or telling them how to do something. "Hold the handle of the cup in your right hand. Dip the cup in the flour. Scrape off the excess with a rubber scraper." That is an example of direct verbal instruction to Samantha in her cake baking lesson.

When you tell five-year-old Sherod, "Don't cross the street because a car is coming," you are teaching him how to cross the street. He has the capacity to learn when to cross the street; he can see the car, he can identify the car, and he can walk across the street. By drawing his attention to the car and reminding him not to cross when he sees a car, you are scaffolding him and thereby assisting his performance in safe street-crossing. You are teaching him!

Less intensive than direct verbal assistance is indirect verbal. Indirect verbal assistance primarily consists of asking questions and giving hints. Teachers call this *probing* and *cueing*. "What does the recipe say to do next?" is a probe. Saying "The eggs need to be..." when Samantha forgets to separate the eggs, is a cue. You are not telling her to separate the eggs, you are giving her a hint that she is supposed to. You are teaching her!

The next least intensive level of assistance is gesturing. When Samantha forgets to add the milk, you can point to the milk. If she no longer needs more intensive assistance, then by this gesture, you have assisted her performance in baking the cake. You are teaching her!

No assistance at all is when she responds to the natural cues, in this case, the recipe card. Now that she no longer needs your assistance, she has left Stage 1, so she will probably talk to herself while she bakes her cakes the next few times. Eventually she will fossilize the skill and can think about other things while she puts her hands on autopilot to prepare the cake.

In addition to Samantha's independent living skills, do you see how these levels of assistance work when you help teach Samantha her homework? Pretty neat, huh?

A final word about teaching independent living skills or homework. Lots of research shows that one-on-one teaching is incredibly powerful in producing student learning. Rich people can afford to pay for any kind of lessons they want, and what they want and pay for is one-on-one teaching. Yet many people discount teaching one-on-one as being somehow less important than teaching a group of students. Thinking that one-on-one teaching is somehow inferior to group instruction is a mistake. It is amazingly, astoundingly, incredibly powerful. So get out there and teach!

In this chapter, we have discussed teaching and learning. We have learned that teaching is assisting performance, we have learned how to scaffold, and we have learned about levels of assistance. In fact, we have probably learned that we have been teaching people things all our lives!

In the next chapter, we will talk about discipline.

Chapter 11

DISCIPLINING KIDS

In the last chapter, we talked about how to teach kids, using Vygotsky's socially mediated apprenticeship theory. In this chapter, we're going to talk about discipline.

What gives houseparents more headaches than disciplining kids? Probably nothing. Of course, the word discipline means to teach, and when we are teaching kids things, we are also teaching them the proper ways to behave as they do those things. But sometimes, kids don't behave like they've been taught to, and that's what I'm talking about here. What then?

In order to think about misbehavior, we need to go back and think about William Glasser's theory of needs. You will remember that we are calling the needs he describes by our F-words: food & fornicating, fun, freedom, force, and family & friends. Glasser explains that what motivates us to do things are these needs. Some of the needs conflict with each other within an individual. For example, the need for family & friends conflicts with the need for freedom within an individual. But one person's needs often conflict with another person's needs (or the needs of a group) and that's where behavior problems come in.

The first thing that we need to try and do when a child is trying to meet his needs in a way that interferes with the needs of others is to help him meet his needs in more appropriate ways. For example, if he is trying to meet his fun need by roughhousing in the living room, we can direct him to go outside to meet that need rather than to punish him. If he is trying to meet his power need by bullying littler kids, we can help him meet that need by putting him in charge of projects so he can meet that need in more constructive ways. If he is trying to meet his friends & family need by sneaking off from chores to play with his friends, we can help him meet that need by pairing him with a friend to get their chores done.

So we're defining *behavior problems* as *when a child meets a need of his in a way that interferes with the needs of others, or when he meets a need in an unsafe way.* As houseparents, we have a need for power (force). Although we may primarily be drawn to houseparenting out of a need for affiliation and belonging (friends & family), we also have a need for power. We have rules and regulations, and it is important to us to see that those rules are followed by the kids in our house. When the kids follow our rules, our power needs are met and we feel good.

When a kid doesn't follow our rules, we say, "He doesn't follow the rules," but what we are actually thinking is, "He is refusing to abide by my authority. He is challenging my power." Because our power need is not being met, we get mad. That's a hard thing to admit, but it's true.

Often, a kid's need for fun, freedom, friends & family, food & fornicating, or power interferes with our need for power. But our cottages *must* have certain rules obeyed in order for us all to be able to live together, in order to assure the health and safety of all the children, and in order to provide an atmosphere that will promote psychological, social, and moral growth. After all, if we let everyone meet all of their needs all of the time in any way they see fit, we'd live in a state of chaos and lawlessness. Bigger kids would beat up littler kids in order to meet their power needs, all kids would swing from the ceiling fans in order to meet their fun needs, and some kids would engage in sexual relations from the time they turned twelve in order to meet their food & fornicating (survival & reproduction) needs.

What I am trying to say here is that we must have reasonable rules, but as we enforce them, we need to keep watch over ourselves in order to be sure that we're acting out of the best interest of all of our entire cottage community and not out of our need for personal power. So let's assume that we've agreed to monitor ourselves to be sure that we're not acting in order to meet our power need under the guise of enforcing necessary rules. So what then?

Let's start with the notion of *restitution vs. retribution.* Restitution means paying back damages done and making right a wrong that was committed. In contrast, retribution means getting even. Don't get me wrong. It feels good to get even. Darn good. It meets our power need. The problem is that getting even with a kid doesn't help him grow.

A startlingly-honest teacher once told me the following story:

> I'm ashamed to admit it, but I get high when I'm chewing a kid out. Especially Hobbie, a first grader, that I had for a short time. When I was giving him what for, I really liked it. It made me ashamed of

myself afterward... What's wrong with me? Why do I get high when I bawl a kid out? And why did I especially like to make Hobby squirm and cry?

Part of what this woman was expressing was that her power need was met by having power over kids in general and over Hobbie in particular.

Early in this book, I told about a young man who intentionally shot the windows out of our barn. I wanted to kill him. At the very least, I wanted to bury him next to an anthill and pour honey over his head. But Kelvin had a cooler head and required restitution instead of retribution. Kelvin required the boy to use his own money to pay the $25 it cost to replace the windows. No more windows got shot out. The boy learned that if he committed a wrong act (or at least this particular wrong act), he had to make it right. It became easier to resist the impulse to shoot the windows out of the barn once he knew that he'd have to pay for new ones. If Kelvin had demanded retribution, the boy would have learned something very different.

What kids learn from retribution is to value getting even. What they learn from restitution is to value making right what they've done wrong. One important part of restitution is understanding how the wrong you have committed affects the person(s) you wronged. When Tim steals David's personal stereo, you need to sit Tim and David down face to face. Then ask David, "How did you feel when Tim stole your stereo?" Tim needs to hear from David how his behavior affected the other boy. Tim also needs to hear how you felt about the incident. By making him hear the perspective of the other people involved in his wrongdoing, Tim begins to learn how to role take, a necessary skill for allowing a person to move beyond Kohlberg's lowest level of moral development.

One disadvantage of punishment is that when kids are punished, they develop an external locus of control. "He made me do it!" is a hallmark of the thinking of kids who are punished. Another disadvantage of punishment is that when kids are punished, they usually get mad and focus their thinking on what a rotten person their punisher is. That's not what we want them to do. What we want them to do is to focus their thinking on their own bad behavior for a while and to make a commitment to themselves to not do the bad thing again.

I tried an experiment on fifteen of my graduate students in counseling and education. I surveyed them about whether they had ever been spanked, and if so, what the results were. In most of the other cases, my students reported that the spankings they received only made them mad at the parent who spanked them. One man said:

> I got spanked for fighting with my brothers and sisters when I was in junior high. All of us were fighting. My dad spanked us all. All it did was make me madder at my brothers and sisters and mad at my dad and God. I was mad at God because my dad was a minister.

The same fellow told me about another spanking he received from his father:

> I was sixteen and I cussed at my mom. Then my dad and I got in a fist fight. He ended up whipping me, and I was scared.

When I asked him if he ever repeated the infractions that lead to these spankings, he said that he did. So the spankings didn't change his behavior. The first one just made him mad at the whole world and God Himself, and the second one only scared him. They didn't make him focus on his behavior and resolve to change it. That's what good discipline does.

A woman recalled being spanked by her parents, and while the spanking did keep her from repeating the infraction, her answer supports the notion that spanking usually makes a child focus on the parent's behavior, rather than her own.

> During church service on a Wednesday night, I held the collection plate as it was being passed down the row—loudly insisting my parents put money in. They didn't have any money with them, so they were upset! They spanked me, and I thought spanking was a little harsh—I really didn't buy that "this hurts me more than it hurts you" line.

If her parents had told her that they were hurt and embarrassed by her behavior, the girl probably would have never repeated the offense, but she also would have learned more, because she would have felt guilty and focused on how her behavior affects others, rather on the behavior of her parents as not telling the truth about "it hurts me more...."

A student wrote of a particular spanking and of spankings in general that she received.

> One time, one of the five of us did something wrong. No one would fess up to it, so we all got spanked. I felt like it wasn't fair. I wasn't the

> one who did it in the first place. But from other spankings: if they were from my mom, it didn't change my behavior. If from my dad, it did. We didn't get spanked often, and when we did it was usually by my dad. I never got a spanking after I turned six or seven.

Although this student didn't elaborate as to why Mom's spankings didn't change her behavior but Dad's did, I wonder if it was because she was frightened of Dad or because she wanted Dad's approval more than she wanted Mom's? We'll talk about that more later.

Another woman told how her thinking focused on how she outsmarted her mother during a spanking.

> My sister and I wouldn't settle down and go to sleep, and after several warnings, my mother came up and spanked us. I was scared it was going to hurt, and when it didn't, I faked cry(ing) so she would stop. I remember thinking (that) I pulled one over on her.

Other students reported that their parents' spankings did not change their behaviors. Only two students clearly indicated that a spanking by their mothers made them make a decision not to repeat the infractions. One of those women wrote:

> I cut my best friend, accidentally, with a pair of pointed scissors which we weren't even supposed to have in the first place and then lied about it. So, I got two spankings, but the one for lying was the worst. I was 9–10 years old. I was glad when it was over, and resolved never to lie again.

The other woman wrote:

> I was shopping with my mom and I was messing around. She told me to stop whatever it was I was doing.... I don't remember now what it was.... But anyway, I didn't stop, so when we got home, she spanked me. I knew I deserved it and my conscience was relieved when she was punishing me. Then I could forget about it and not feel bad any more.

Of all the spankings reported by the fifteen students, only these two spankings yielded the desired results. And remember that these spankings were all administered by the children's parents, the source of all love to a child.

But I was especially interested in what the students remembered about being spanked by someone other than their own mom and dad, because as houseparents, as much as we like to think that the kids in our homes think of us as their parents, we know that they don't. "You're not my mom!" or "You're not my dad!" is a phrase we hear thrown in our faces all too often. I think we can draw better inferences about what kids think about being spanked by houseparents when we look at comments about being spanked by teachers, since kids don't consider either the houseparent or the teacher as "my real parent."

The same woman who reported that she had been spanked for misbehaving while shopping reported that she had been spanked by her first grade teacher for talking. As in the earlier example, she reported that she never repeated the infraction, that she thought she deserved to be spanked, and that she was glad it was over. Hers was the only response that indicated that a spanking by a teacher had the desired results.

A man wrote the following.

> I got spanked twice in school, once in first grade, and once in junior high. The teacher spanked me in first grade, and the administrator in junior high. The deal in first grade was because several of us boys were throwing spitwads in class when the teacher was out. She walked in during our play. She took us in the hallway, lined us up, walked outside and broke a branch off the tree, and came in and swatted us. . . . It was an adventure and I prayed they did not tell my parents. . . . It didn't keep me from doing it again, I just got smarter and didn't get caught.

So this man didn't change his naughty behavior; he simply resolved to be sneakier about it.

One man reported that he was spanked once or twice each year in junior high school, and while he did focus on his behavior after the spanking, he did repeat the offense.

> I had fairly good relationships with my teachers. My English teacher, my P. E. teacher, and my math teacher all paddled me. I would get to the point where I became an annoyance to the teacher. I was an A student. I was spanked for continually speaking out during inappropriate times in class and having other kids laugh when the teacher was trying to teach. After being spanked by the teacher, I felt sad, alone, and as if I had let him down. . . . I thought I let myself down and my classmates and my teacher. . . . I was sad and felt alone. . . .

His desire for fun and for friends & family drove him to repeat his offenses even after being spanked at least twice.

A woman reported that she had been spanked at school. I don't know how the teacher saw the situation, but the woman believed that she was spanked for not understanding the lesson. She wrote, "I felt the spanking was not deserving (sic)." If I were spanked for not understanding a lesson, I would think it wasn't deserved, either. But was that really the teacher's reason for spanking the student? Maybe, or maybe not. We'll probably never know. I suspect that we often paddle kids for one thing and they think it's for something else entirely.

In a similar vein, a woman wrote:

> I got spanked in school two times: fifth grade and twelfth grade. In fifth grade, the principal spanked me for running on the sidewalk. I was embarrassed. I was a quiet child and had A's in conduct. This was probably my only interaction with her. In twelfth grade, the dean of women in high school for some reason tried to "catch" me doing something wrong for years. Two days before graduation, she caught me skipping a class. I had to take licks or not graduate. The lady was a witch! Again I did not have the reputation of being a troublemaker. I was embarrassed, but to save face, I said, "Thank you very much," and I didn't tear up until I left the office—it hurt! I didn't repeat the behavior because I graduated two days later, but I would have just because the dean was such a biased witch.

In both of these situations, the student clearly felt that her punishment was undeserved. Her focus was on the unjust behavior of the administrator, not on her own behavior.

It is important to note that these students are all highly educated people who were successful in school. It is also important to note that all but two of them do approve of corporal punishment. Yet even by their own admission, only one student, the lady who had been spanked in first grade, indicated that the spanking clearly accomplished what it was intended to: to make her think about her behavior and resolve not to commit the offense again. In every other case, the spanking either didn't accomplish its aims because the behavior was repeated, or resulted in the student focusing on the teacher's behavior rather than on his or her own behavior.

If we do decide that punishment, rather than restitution, is in order, let's keep several things in mind. First, if a child is at Kohlberg's pleasure vs. pain stage, then it may be that punishment, rather than restitution, is the only thing that will work with him. But if we do punish, we are better off punishing the child in a non-physical way if we can. When we punish a child by inflicting physical pain, we are teaching him to settle his differences with others by inflicting physical pain on them. We can punish him by taking away privileges or by grounding him. I personally don't like assigning a child extra work in order to punish him; I think that being a hard worker is really important, and if I use work to punish kids, then I teach them that work is punishment, not pleasure. I want kids to learn to think of work as pleasurable, so I'd never use it as punishment.

In contrast, working to make restitution is a different matter entirely. Then, I am working (a good thing) to make right what I did wrong; I am not working as a punishment, because work is a bad thing to have to do.

The one time when punishment in the form of spanking is probably called for is when a child at the pleasure-pain level is engaging in dangerous activity. For example, when we see two-year-old Adrian crawling over the fence to go out in the street, spanking is probably called for. A swift swat or two on the bottom should be sufficient, because it's not the pain itself but the intense displeasure of his caretaker that is important. If I never spank Adrian, but under these circumstances I do, coupled with a voice and facial expression that communicate great displeasure, then he may be dissuaded from repeating the infraction. Certainly, he's too young to be reasoned with, and in order to control his fun and freedom needs that spur him to climb the fence, I have to make his need for parental approval (friends & family) so great that he will sacrifice the fun and freedom that fence-climbing would provide. That I would strike him is such a rare thing, that he will know that fence-climbing is verboten.

Do you remember the woman who said that her mother's spankings didn't change her behavior but that her father's spankings did? It may be that Dad's spankings changed her behavior because he spanked harder than Mom did, but I doubt it. I suspect that Dad expressed greater disapproval of her bad behavior than Mom did and that it was more important to her to please Dad than it was to please Mom. Therefore, when Dad spanked her, she resolved never to repeat the offense again because she wanted him to approve of her. In contrast, it wasn't as important to please Mom, and besides, Mom didn't seem as upset when she spanked as Dad did when he spanked.

Case in point. I was spanked twice during my school career and both spankings were on the same day. I was in the eighth grade, and I went in after school to ask my science teacher to show me my grade average. He was a man whom I admired, but he was a quirky guy, so when I asked him about my grade, he ignored me and continued doing whatever it was that he was doing. I asked again and he continued to ignore me. About the third time I asked, I saw his paddle lying under some papers on his desk and I said, "If you don't answer me, I'm going to hit you in the back of your head with your paddle."

He didn't answer me, so I picked up the paddle and popped him in the back of the neck with it. Of course, I had no idea of the physical damage that could have caused, and I thank God to this day that he was unhurt. But he was mightily displeased. He jumped up, bent me over his desk, and wore me out with self-same paddle. I cried and wailed, not so much because it hurt, although it did, but because I had made him angry.

Now the second spanking happened because of the first spanking. Our band director had an ironclad rule that if a member of the band were spanked by any other teacher, they would also be spanked by him, no questions asked. He said, "You are ambassadors of the band, and whenever you bring shame to yourself, you bring shame to all of us." So we understood and respected this rule and felt that it was fair.

Now, I would have never in a gazillion years have told my band director about being spanked by my science teacher, but as luck would have it, (unbeknownst to me) John, our drum major, walked by the door as I was being spanked and saw the whole thing. A real law & order kind of guy, John couldn't wait to report me to our band director.

Well, I dried my eyes and pulled myself together after my spanking and went out to the bandhall. There, in the office, stood John and my band director, who was holding his paddle. From the look on his face, I could tell that my band director was ticked off big time. All he said to me was, "I don't care what you did or didn't do. No excuses. I don't even want to hear about it. Bend over and grab the edge of the desk." I did and then he whopped me good. I cried again, but as before, it wasn't the sting of the paddle that made me cry. What made me cry was that I had made my band director mad at me. I would rather have had twelve Hell's Angels run over me with their motorcycles than have ticked him off.

On that day, then, began and ended my short career of violence. I resolved never to hit anyone again with anything for the rest of my life (to this moment). And it was not because of the physical pain of the spanking that I made that resolution, it was because my actions resulted in the displeasure of a teacher whom I admired and of a second teacher whom I adored. It would have been just as effective (maybe more so) if the first teacher had sat me down and told me how angry and disappointed that he was in me. As it was, although it stopped that behavior once and for all, the spankings also served to relieve me of guilt: I had paid for my crime. Had I not felt as though I had done penance, then I would have continued to feel guilt for my actions and think about them for days to come, perhaps a far better result.

It's like this: You can spank a dog with a rolled-up newspaper, which doesn't hurt at all, and change its behavior because it is horrified to have displeased you. In the same way, if you decide that you must spank a child to stop dangerous behavior, then a couple of swats with the bare hand will do it. It's your displeasure that makes the child want to change his behavior.

Although we might decide that spanking is in order once in a great while, we need to keep in mind that many of our kids come to us having been abused. It's not a good idea to ever use physical punishment on a kid who has spent his life getting beat up by his parents. If we spank this kid, we are just confirming to him that might is right and that whatever force you use to get your way, that's okay, because that's how you get things done.

Let's also keep in mind two cardinal rules about spanking:
1. NEVER SPANK A CHILD WHEN YOU ARE ANGRY.
2. MAKE SURE THAT YOU ARE SPANKING THE CHILD FOR HIS SAKE AND NOT FOR YOUR SAKE.

So we've agreed that restitution is almost always better than retribution, and that if we decide that actual punishment is necessary, then non-physical punishment is better than physical punishment. We've also discussed that if physical punishment is necessary, such as dealing with a pleasure-pain level child who is engaging in very dangerous activity, then it's not the amount of pain that changes behavior, it is the expression of severe disapproval. So that brings to the question of what is the best style of parental control in order to help kids grow up into self-disciplined adults?

There are three basic parenting styles. The first style is the *authoritarian* style. Authoritarian parents try to keep constant control over the behavior of their kids. Rules are set in stone and must be followed without question. They stress obedience and punishment, and often spank their kids. They have high power needs and receive great satisfaction from forcing kids to follow rules. Authoritarian parents also often use withdrawal of love as a punishment. People who use an authoritarian style have been found in experiments to have a high need to dominate people and to be unhealthily rigid and inflexible. Too many houseparents are authoritarian-style parents.

Permissive parents, on the other hand, don't punish their kids and accept many behaviors that the other two types of parents would not condone. The permissive parent talks with the child about bad behaviors. He explains why a rule exists and reasons with his child about why a rule should be followed. In fact, reason, rather than punishment, is the central tenet of the permissive parent's parenting style. Not too many houseparents are permissive types.

The third style is the one that has been most successful in creating kids who are cooperative, independent, friendly, and hard workers. This style is the *authoritative* style. The authoritative style parent directs his child through reason (like the permissive parent), rather than punishment (like the authoritarian parent), but not on the basis of equality (unlike the permissive parent). He uses firm, rather than dictatorial (like the authoritarian parent), control. His central tenet is explaining rules (like the permissive parent) but enforcing them even if the child doesn't agree that they are fair (like the authoritarian parent). This is a parent who has struck a healthy balance between the other two parenting types and who has his power need firmly under his own control; he doesn't need to intimidate kids. He sets reasonable rules and is fair and consistent about enforcing them.

In this chapter, we have talked about the notion of misbehavior as a child's attempt to meet his Glasserian needs in a way which interferes with the needs of others. We determined that the best way to handle behavior problems is to help a child meet his needs in more acceptable ways. We also talked about the notion of restitution vs. retribution and determined that it is better to teach a child to fix the wrong he has done rather for us to get even with him. We also talked about punishment in general, and spanking in particular, as not being very effective. However, we noted that in specific cases in which we do use spanking, that it is the extreme disapproval of the parental figure in the situation that is the key to changing a child's behavior. Finally, we identified three parenting styles, authoritarian, permissive, and authoritative, and determined that the authoritative style is best in helping us produce the kinds of kids that we want to produce.

In the next chapter, we will discuss the problems unique to people who live in the fishbowl that we call a group home.

Chapter 12

LIVING IN A FISHBOWL

In the last chapter, we talked about ways of disciplining children. In this chapter, we are going to move away from childrearing as such and talk about some problems that are rather unique to houseparents.

The first problem I want to talk about is how having a lot of people living in one house affects us. We'll start by thinking about the science of proxemics, or the science of how people utilize space.

People from different cultures use space differently. People who are enculturated as African American or Hispanic use space differently than people who are enculturated into the white culture. This different use of space can cause misunderstandings.

Let me start by explaining the way that people in the white culture use space.

There are four spatial zones that surround a person. The most immediate zone is called *intimate space*. Intimate space ranges from body contact to about eighteen inches. The only people that we naturally feel comfortable having face-to-face with us in our intimate space are our lover or our child. Under formal circumstances in their role as healers, we are comfortable allowing our physician, nurse, or other healers, in our personal space; however, if our healer tries to get into our personal space while we are talking with him informally at the mall, we won't like it one bit.

We are so protective of our intimate space that I have heard it said that if you see two unmarried adults sharing intimate space face-to-face, then you can be sure that they either just finished having intercourse or are getting ready to.

Sometimes, however, we are forced to share intimate space. What then?

If we are forced to share intimate space, we engage in very formalized rituals in order to pretend like we don't know the other person is there. Think of the last time that you rode in a crowded elevator. Everyone faced the front, didn't they? No one turned around to stand face-to-face with anyone else. If someone bumped you with their briefcase, you pretended not to notice, didn't you? You pretended like the bumper wasn't there.

Even if you were talking to someone before you entered the elevator, you probably stopped talking when you got on. If you did continue talking, you didn't face your conversation partner to talk, and you probably felt awkward talking at all, although you may have forced yourself to.

One exception to the intimacy rule occurs when you want to tell a naughty joke to a friend or share a secret or a juicy bit of gossip. Under these conditions, you will feel comfortable entering your friend's intimate space almost face-to-face. But once the joke/secret/gossip is told, you move right back out of intimate space.

Another exception to the intimate space rule occurs when you are greeting a friend whom you haven't seen in a while, bidding farewell to a friend you don't plan to see again for a while, and when you are comforting a bereaved friend.

We even move into face-to-face intimate space with strangers when we are comforting them. For example, if you see an injured person lying on the highway, you don't hesitate to move into his intimate space. Even if the medics are there taking care of the injured person, you feel quite comfortable holding someone who is grieving over the injured person. For example, if a man is injured and being attended to by paramedics, you wouldn't feel awkward holding and comforting his wife.

Other than these situations, we typically don't want anyone face-to-face with us in our intimate space. And even in these situations, although we may not mind our bodies facing each other, we still avoid our faces facing each other.

Note that we are much more comfortable having someone side-to-side with us in intimate space than we are face-to-face. For example, we can sit right next to a friend in a crowded car and not necessarily be uncomfortable. However, we would be uncomfortable sitting right next to our friend if the car weren't crowded. But in any event, we are more comfortable side-to-side in intimate space than we are face-to-face.

From eighteen inches to about four feet is our *personal space.* In this space, we typically want our friends and pleasant acquaintances. Tables in bars and restaurants are built in order to allow us to engage in face-to-face interaction with our friends in our personal space. Lounging areas in the lobbies of hotels are typically arranged in conversation groups which place parties in a group within four feet of each other.

Do some of your friends have homes that you naturally feel comfortable in? You go over for an evening of food and conversation and feel so comfortable there, but you can't exactly explain why? In contrast, do you have friends with whom you feel as close as you do the friends in the previous question, yet when you go to their homes for an evening, you don't feel as comfortable? It may well be because the first set of friends have their furniture arranged so that you share personal space, while the second set of friends have their furniture arranged so that you are outside of personal space with each other.

I used to live in a house with a greatroom. I placed the couch against one wall and the two recliners against the opposite wall. To one side of these pieces of furniture, I placed a chair and ottoman. It looked okay, but when people came over, it didn't feel right. I didn't know why. I thought it was because the room was so big.

In contrast, I could go to the homes of some of my friends, and even if they had a greatroom, the room felt cozy and inviting. I couldn't figure it out.

After I learned about proxemics, I made sure to arrange my furniture so that at least one chair sat in a conversational grouping with the couch, and preferably, both chairs did. Presto-chango, immediately the atmosphere of the room changed.

Nowadays, when I go to a friend's house, if her furniture isn't arranged in conversational groupings, I have to bite my tongue not to tell her all about how she ought to rearrange her furniture to place people in each other's personal space.

One interesting activity that involves personal space and has its own special rules is using urinals in a public restroom. This activity was studied and reported by the anthropologist, Eliott Oring.

> One's personal space during urination extends to one urinal to the left and right of the pee-er and therefore a minimum one-urinal distance between oneself and fellow pee-ers should be maintained whenever possible. Thus if urinal 1 is occupied, theoretically, urinals 3, 4 and 5 are available. If 3 is occupied, 1 and 5 are available. Of course, if the only unoccupied urinals are adjacent to other pee-ers they may be selected. But if there are any isolated urinals, they must be filled before urinals adjacent to other pee-ers can be used. There are some individuals who will not violate peeing space even when the only urinals available are adjacent to other pee-ers and will wash their hands or comb their hair until the distribution of people changes sufficiently

to allow them their personal space. Others will simply use the stalls when they feel their personal space cannot be guaranteed. (Oring, 1979, p. 17)

Oring goes on to explain that:

The violation of the principle of personal peeing space regularly occurs in only one situation. One may stand adjacent to another pee-er, with other urinals available, only when that person is known. Conversation invariably develops between these individuals. Such conversation is often phatic and serves to demonstrate the existence of a prior social relationship rather than to convey specific information. All conversations in men's rooms are loud and can be heard by all present. There is no attempt at whispered or surreptitious communication. (Oring, 1979, p. 18)

I don't know that this information will ever be of much use to you, but I thought it was interesting and it certainly illustrates the notion of personal space.

From four to twelve feet is our *social space*. We use social space for business and impersonal transactions. For example, the clerk behind the counter at the grocery store typically stands four feet away from us. The guy behind the lemonade stand typically stands four feet away from us. And the lady at the chicken place who fills our order typically stands four feet away from us. In the same way that it's not a coincidence that tables at restaurants and bars place you in personal space, it's not a coincidence that counters at businesses place you in social space. The designers know about proxemics and they design their products to place people who use them in the proper space with those with whom they interact.

Public space is anything beyond twelve feet. Professors typically stand at the front of the class, twelve or more feet from the first row. Actors play out their roles on a stage twelve or more feet from the audience. And the minister at church stands behind a pulpit twelve or more feet from the congregation.

You may think, "Well, the minister only stands up there so that everyone can see him." I think that everyone could see him if he came out from behind the pulpit and stood right in front of the people on the front row. But he doesn't because that would make those people feel uncomfortable. When the preacher started talking about fornicating and committing adultery, the folks on the front row would start squirming, because they would think that he was talking about them. So he stays up there behind the pulpit and keeps everyone in the congregation in his public space.

These proxemics rules are those that govern our actions as people who are acculturated into white American culture. These rules don't necessarily apply to other groups.

For example, both African American and Hispanic persons tend to employ closer proxemics than Caucasians do. Friends may more quickly enter into intimate space and strangers may more quickly enter into personal space if the interactors share the African American or Hispanic cultures. This can cause misunderstandings when the interactors are from differing cultural groups.

For example, if an African American and a Caucasian are interacting, if the duo are in the Caucasian's comfortable space for that interaction, they may be too far apart for the African American to be comfortable. Therefore, the African American may move closer to become more comfortable. This, in turn, makes the Caucasian uncomfortable, so he backs away. The African American may interpret the Caucasian's behavior as aloof and unfriendly, while the Caucasian may interpret the African American's behavior as pushy and aggressive. Neither one is being either; both of them are just trying to get comfortable in the interaction.

There is an old joke in sociology that if you place an Arab (very close personal space) in a room with an Englishman (very far personal space), the Arab will keep moving closer to the Englishman, who in turn will keep backing away, until the Englishman ends up against the wall, and as the Arab moves closer to him once again, the Englishman will either scream and faint or bolt and flee.

In our cottages, problems with personal space are evident when a kid screams at us, "Get outta my face!" Typically, when we get in Billy's face, we are chewing him out. He's ticked off because we are telling him what to do or not do, or we are criticizing something that he already did, so he's upset to begin with. But then we compound Billy's anger by moving into his personal space and therefore violating it.

That's also why when men are driving their cars, they become so upset when someone cuts in front of them. It's not only that the person is in front of them that upsets a man driver, it's also because he feels like his space has been violated. (However, men *don't* like the people in the car ahead, because to men, driving is a competitive activity.)

Indeed, by claiming someone's space, we are claiming power over them. We actively move into Billy's space when we chew him out so that we are in a position of power. (Not that we consciously do this, because most of us don't realize why we are doing it.)

But when so many people live together, as we do in children's homes, we are going to inadvertently have problems of people invading each other's space. While some of those problems will be related to the invasion of normal body space (we're invading Billy's space as we chew him out, or Jose invades Billy's space because they come from cultures that use space differently), some of those problems will be related to the invasion of abnormal body space.

Abnormal body space refers to the proxemics of people who are violent. Studies have been conducted of the proxemics of violent criminals, and from those studies, we have learned that people who are violent have abnormally distant body territories and that they react with abnormal intensity when their spaces are violated. For example, whereas you and I have an intimate space of zero to eighteen inches, a violent person may have intimate space of four feet. Therefore, when you move into your personal zone with this guy, you are violating his intimate space and he'll pop you in the nose. Or worse.

Needless to say, some of the kids that you and I raise have violent histories. "He asked for it!" argues Alan after he has popped little PeeWee. "He keeps getting in my face and bugging me!" PeeWee, much younger and smaller, is bewildered. He didn't know that he was getting in Alan's face. He was just wandering through the room and asked Alan what he was doing. But in spite of the lack of intent on PeeWee's part, Alan felt violated.

Another way that we can invade another person's space is by invading his private living area. We all have what is known as front stage and back stage areas in our living quarters. Our front stage areas are typically our living and dining areas, and a bathroom that is placed so that company uses it. Our back stage areas are our bedrooms, closets, personal bathrooms, and perhaps our kitchen. When a guest goes into one of these rooms without being invited, we are upset. We may not even understand why we feel this way.

Margurite told me this story:

> I invited a couple and their little boy over for dinner. After dinner, we went into the living room. Their little boy was playing with some toys I found for him, until he had to go to the bathroom. He was gone a long time, but I didn't think anything about it. Well, after

> while, his mom and I got to talking about quilts, and I went back to my bedroom to get my grandmother's quilt to show her, and there was the little brat, looking around in my closet! I wanted to throttle him! It was completely irrational of me to be so angry. I don't know why I got so mad, but I jerked him up and marched him out to his folks and told them that he was in my bedroom closet. It ruined the whole evening. They took him and left. I don't know why I overreacted like that.

Margurite didn't really overreact. Whenever someone goes back stage without an invitation, we feel violated.

Areas that are highly populated, such as group homes, may have front stage and back stage areas differentiated even more rigidly than homes that are not so densely populated. If the only place in the home that is a back stage for Barry is his dresser, then violation of that space will make him wild.

Angie told me this story about the kids in her cottage:

> Jeff gets so mad when (his roommate) Terry borrows one of his tapes. I can't understand it. The stereo is Terry's, and Terry lets Jeff use it whenever he wants, but Jeff won't let Terry borrow his tapes without permission. You'd think that Jeff would be glad to share tapes with Terry, since Terry shares his stereo with Jeff.

What Angie didn't understand was the notion of back stage and front stage areas. The stereo sat on the table between the two boys' twin beds. The bedside table was front stage, and since the crowded room allowed for only one stereo, and Terry's was the better of the two boys' stereos, its placement on front stage made it public property.

In contrast, each boy's dresser was back stage. Since Jeff kept his tapes on the top of his dresser, Terry's getting one of the tapes off of the dresser constituted a spacial violation.

A spacial issue that causes problems between kids and houseparents, rather than between kids and other kids, is how bedrooms are decorated. Most group homes prohibit the posting of pictures of nude people, and kids generally accept that. But kids often place other posters on the wall that their houseparents find offensive. These can range from pictures of not-quite-nude thong-clad beach bums to those hideous blood-dripping skull posters that kids are so crazy about.

By decorating his room with posters, Jeff is symbolically claiming his space. In the same way, when I moved into the house that I am currently renting, the very first thing that I unpacked was my paintings and framed prints. I had them hung before I even unpacked the box that held the toilet paper. It was my way of taking this space that belongs to someone else and symbolically claiming it for my own.

When a youngster decorates his room, he is symbolically carving out a space that is his own. I think that this act of space-claiming is particularly crucial when you move into a home that is not yours. You feel out of control when you don't have a place of your own; having a place of your own gives you power, and as you will remember, power is one of our motivating needs identified by Glasser.

Next, let's look specifically at issues of overcrowding.

The earliest studies of overcrowding were conducted with rats. Researchers gradually increased the number of rats that lived in a cage. At some point, the rats reached a population density that was unacceptable to them. Once that level was reached, the rats began to attack each other. The previously rather peaceful rats killed each other and even ate their own young. In addition, the female rats quit having babies altogether.

Some folks think that the lemings that periodically rush headlong into the sea do so because they have reached a population density that they can't stand. They solve their overpopulation problem by committing mass suicide.

Crowding itself is a psychological state. For example, I thoroughly enjoy myself in a busy mall, while my husband is losing his mind. "Let's get out of here! It's too crowded!" he barks at me as I check out one last book before I can leave the bookstore. A level of population density that I find exhilarating, he finds intolerable.

In 1973, researchers named Valins and Baum studied the effects of crowding in college dormitories. The dorms studied were of two very different designs. One set of dorms were corridors with long hallways, off of which branched seventeen rooms with two people per room. These dorms had a shared bathroom and lounge. The other dorms were suites of six students each. Each suite had a shared bathroom and lounge. There were several suites per floor, but the effect of the suite dorms was one of being much less crowded than the corridor dorms.

First, the researchers surveyed the students in order to find out whether they felt too crowded in their dorms. In the corridor dorms, 67% of the residents felt too crowded as compared to only 25% of the residents of the suite dorms.

In another study of the effects of crowding, a researcher named Bickman compared the moral behavior of students living in highly populated dorms (500 residents), moderately populated dorms (165 residents), and sparsely populated dorms (58 students). Bickman used what is called the lost-letter technique. The lost-letter technique involves leaving a stamped, addressed envelope on the floor where someone will find it. The envelope does not have a return address. The experiment was designed to make the letter finder think that someone in the dorm had dropped the letter on their way to the mailbox.

Bickman found that the more highly populated the dorm, the less likely the letter finder was to mail the letter. In the sparsely populated dorm, 100% of the letters were mailed. In the moderately populated dorm, 87% of the letters were mailed. And in the highly populated dorm, only 63% of the letters were mailed. This suggests that the more highly populated an area is, the less likely the residents are to engage in moral helping behavior.

One explanation to why people behave less morally in crowded conditions is the need for privacy. Privacy is defined as controlling boundaries so that we can limit other people's access to us. When we cannot control who has access to us, we develop a feeling of helplessness, or as Glasser would say, loss of control.

Another explanation was given by the very controversial Robert Ardrey in his books written in the 1960s. Ardrey argued that like many animals, man had an innate need for territory and that this need to control territory was what led humankind to engage in war. Ardrey suggested that the population problem would control itself, as we would engage in war in order to re-establish healthy numbers of inhabitants when our numbers became too great. In all fairness to Ardrey, he wasn't promoting war but was rather arguing that war would be the result of not limiting our population growth.

Since many of our group homes are overcrowded, is it any wonder that we have kids who fight at the drop of a hat?

A number of things contribute to our psychological sense of crowdedness. The shape of a room can make us feel crowded. The amount and arrangement of the furniture can make us feel crowded. Even the color of the walls or the number of windows can make us feel crowded.

As houseparents we can't change the size of our rooms, but we can change the arrangement of the furniture. We probably can't change the number of windows, but we probably can change the color of the walls.

And there are environmental variables that we can change more easily than that.

Two important environmental variables that affect whether or not we feel crowded are temperature and noise. The hotter we are, the more crowded we feel. Feeling hot and crowded makes us feel aggressive. Policemen can tell you that violent crime goes up during the heat of the summer and goes down in the cooler months. Many of our children's home administrators tell us to keep the air conditioner set so as to keep the utilities down, but we do so at the risk of increasing problems within our cottages.

Noise is defined as an unwanted sound, and noise can make us feel crowded. However, for some reason that I do not understand, most kids don't seem to be very bothered by noise. We houseparents are the ones that feel crowded in a noisy environment. Hearing rock music makes me feel crowded anytime, and even music that I would otherwise enjoy makes me feel crowded when my husband wants to listen to it in the middle of the night. I also feel crowded when he turns on radio talk shows in the middle of the night. Suddenly, the walls start closing in on me and I want to run screaming out into the street.

Since noise doesn't seem to crowd kids but does crowd us adults, maybe a good solution is for children's homes to provide earplugs for houseparents.

Another thing that is related to living in a densely populated cottage is what is called "worst kid syndrome." This means that there will always be one kid who drives you crazy. You start obsessing on this kid and think, "If I could only get Steve out of my cottage, everything would be great."

Day and night you think about how much better life would be without Steve. Every time he breaks a rule or talks back, you think, "If I could only get rid of that one kid...." Little by little, his good qualities become fainter and his bad qualities become more pronounced until you are living and breathing Steve and trying to figure out how to get rid of him.

Finally the day comes that he crosses the line and is sent away to a detention hall. Or maybe he requests and gets a transfer to another cottage. Or maybe he finally gets to go home. Whatever the reason, he's gone and you breathe a huge sigh of relief.

But not for long. Because guess what? The kid who was the next to the worst kid in your cottage suddenly becomes the new worst kid. Now it is

Bart that you begin obsessing on, thinking, "If I could only get rid of Bart, this cottage would be perfect." But it wouldn't, because every time a worst kid leaves, then the next to the worst kid automatically becomes the worst kid.

The key to stopping yourself from falling prey to the worst kid syndrome is knowing that it exists. Now that you know it exists, when Steve does something that makes you mad and you start thinking, "If I could only get rid of Steve," stop yourself and chuckle. Realize that there's always going to be a worse kid in your cottage, and if they all moved away except for Gabriel the Archangel, then you would start thinking of old Gabriel himself as the worst kid in the cottage.

The last thing that I want to mention in this chapter is living with another set of houseparents. It is hard enough to agree with your spouse on how kids ought to be raised. It is almost impossible to agree with two people who aren't even related to you about how to best raise kids. I am convinced that the number one cause of houseparent turnover is related less to problems with the kids than to problems with the other houseparents.

We don't know all the answers to solving the problem of living with another set of adults, but we will try to offer some solutions in the next chapter on communication skills, and then more solutions will be offered in the chapter on conflict resolution skills.

In this chapter, we have discussed some of the problems of living in a fishbowl. We looked at the use of personal space, at the effects of crowding, and at the worst kid syndrome. We also noted that often the most challenging problem in being a houseparent is not the kids but living with another set of houseparents. In the next chapter, we'll tell you about some communication skills that may help.

Chapter 13

COMMUNICATING BETTER WITH KIDS AND CO-WORKERS

In the last chapter, we talked about life in a fishbowl and how having a bunch of people living together in one house can create problems. In this chapter, we are going to talk about improving communication so that we can better deal with the problems of being one goldfish in a whole school of goldfish.

"It's not so much what he says as the way he says it!" Sherilyn told me of Don, the senior housedad in the cottage in which she and her husband were junior houseparents. "He is such an annoying person to have to work with! He always makes me feel like a second class citizen...."

The fact that it ain't so much whatcha say, as the way ya say it, is the cause of a lot of problems in living and working in such close quarters with so many other people. This way ya say it is what linguists call *nonverbal communication,* or *NVC.*

Maybe the one most important forms of NVC is making comfortable eye contact with the other person. Although there are cultural differences about eye contact, generally speaking this helps another person to talk with us if we look at their face in a way that's comfortable: not staring or glaring but simply occasionally making direct eye contact with them by allowing them to look into our eyes as they are comfortable. If I want to help you talk and I'm looking in the general direction of your face, then when you look to my eyes, they say, "I am paying attention to you. I value you, and I want to hear what you have to say."

Two important cultural differences need to be noted here. First, kids enculturated in the Hispanic culture learn that it is disrespectful to have eye contact with an authority. So when an Anglo houseparent is scolding a Hispanic child, the child doesn't look in the houseparent's eyes. "Look at me when I'm talking to you!" is a command that is frequently overheard when white houseparents are speaking to Hispanic kids. The houseparent interprets the lack of eye contact as defiance; the child is not being defiant according to his cultural norms. He is behaving properly. The skill of interpreting a person's behavior from the point of view of his culture is called cultural relativity.

A second difference is the eye contact used in the African American culture. Now follow carefully. When Anglo people talk, the listener looks into the eyes of the speaker more frequently, and the speaker looks into the eyes of the listener less frequently. When African Americans talk, the speaker looks into the eyes of the listener more frequently, and the listener looks into the eyes of the speaker less frequently. The cultures are opposite from each other in this way. But in either culture, it's like a dance. We're looking at each other in order to show our interest, but not to the point where we appear to be staring. Staring is considered hostile.

Now here's the problem. When a white person and an African American person are talking to each other, the white speaker thinks the African American listener is not paying attention, because the African American person is not looking at the white speaker as often as the white speaker thinks he should be looked at. In contrast, when the African American person is speaking, he thinks the white person is hostile, because the white person is looking at him more often than he believes is appropriate.

Another important part of NVC is the way we use proxemics, the use of space which we described in the last chapter. For example, we move in closer when we talk to people if we want to create a feeling of closeness with them. We move farther away if we want to create a feeling of aloofness.

That's one of the things that I noticed about Don, once I started watching the interactions that he had with Sherilyn: he always kept a greater distance between himself and her when they talked than I knew she would have preferred. Sherilyn was a warm and bubbly woman, who touched people a lot as she talked with them, so it was also her instinct to move in closely to people when she was talking with them. Don kept moving away, sort of like the old story of the Englishman and the Arab we talked about in the last chapter.

Since I knew that Sherilyn was a toucher, I asked her if she had ever touched Don while she was talking to him. "Are you kidding?" she asked. "I wouldn't dare!"

I used this opening to tell Sherilyn about *haptics,* or the study of the use of touch.

Like our use of proxemics, our use of haptics is an important method of NVC. We can communicate all kinds of things by the way we use touch.

For example, when you have a friend who has just lost a spouse or a child, you probably hug them. You don't even have to say a word; the hug says it all: *I'm sorry, and I'm here for you.* When you attend your child's first school operetta and she runs to you grinning ear to ear after the performance, you grab her up in a big hug. You don't have to say, "You did great! I am so proud of you!" The hug says it for you. (But it would be nice if you said the words, too.)

Likewise, if you reach your hand under the table and caress the back of your honey's knee, you have effectively communicated a message that wouldn't be confused with either of the previous examples.

Touch is so important in communication that when I was about six years old, my dad taught me "the right way" to shake hands.

"Shake hands with a strong, hard grip," he said. "People will judge your character by the strength of your handshake."

So I started shaking hands like a visegrip. Grown men would invariably look amused when they shook hands with this tiny girl who gripped their big paws like a pro wrestler. "That's quite a grip you have there, young lady," they would say, and I'd smile back, because I knew then that they thought I was a person of character.

Ever since then, I have been highly suspicious of people who offer me weak handshakes, unless I know that they have arthritis. Even though I know that most middle class women have been socialized to give soft handshakes, I prefer to shake hands with a woman who gives me a good, sturdy handshake in return.

Another kind of NVC involves the use of gestures.

One of the most effective gestures at encouraging or discouraging a feeling of interest in a speaker is how you hold your arms. If you want to show interest in the speaker, don't cross your arms across your chest. Folding your arms across your chest is one of the gestures referred to as closed body language; you are closing yourself off from the speaker.

It is easier to keep an open arm position when you are seated than when you are standing. Seated, you can put your arms on the arms of the chair, rest your chin on the edge of your fist, or do a number of other natural-looking things. It's a little harder to be standing in a conversation that lasts more than a sentence or two and find something natural-looking to do with your hands unless you are holding something. However, if you want to create an atmosphere of openness, it's important that you don't cross your arms.

Crossing his arms when Sherilyn tried talking to him was one of the gestures that I noticed that Don used, once I started consciously watching to see the two of them interact. His crossed arms contrasted sharply with her open body language, and I could see why she had learned not to like him and to think that he was aloof. (I also thought that he looked defensive, since crossing our arms across our chest is one of the things that we do when we are defensive.)

In addition to having an open or closed chest because of the way of positioning your arms, crossing your legs can also make your conversation partner feel like you are disinterested or defensive. Most of us cross our legs during a large part of our conversations when we are not sitting with our feet under a table or desk, so we may have to consciously work at keeping them uncrossed. One of the things that I do when I want to show my openness and interest to a conversational partner is tuck one foot under my chair and place the other forward. It sounds awkward but comes across as looking interested and non-defensive.

Another NVC trick to appearing interested is leaning slightly forward in your chair toward your listener. Sherilyn wouldn't have known why, but if Don had leaned slightly toward her when she talked rather than away from her, she wouldn't have felt nearly so rejected by him.

Other gestures such as head nodding or shaking tell a lot about what we feel. Or at least send messages which others interpret as revealing what we feel.

A memorable example from my own life occurred when I was being interviewed for admission to the doctoral program at the University of Arkansas. I entered the room to find five people waiting for me. I was scared silly anyway, but when I was talking about a professor that I had known at another university years ago, one of my interviewers started shaking his head. I thought that he meant that I was lying, that I did not know the professor who I was talking about, and I started saying, "Well, maybe I didn't get her name right," stumbling all over myself.

After I left the interview and had time to calm down, I knew that I had gotten her name right. I later learned that he had attended the university around the time that I had been there and that he did not know her, so was shaking his head trying to remember her being there. Nevertheless, I had responded strongly to his NVC and I felt like he thought I was lying.

Just as head shaking sends negative messages to our conversation partner, head nodding sends positive messages. Maybe that's why I always smile when I see a car with one of those little head-bobbing dogs in the rear window of their car. It makes me feel like it likes me.

The people I know who most consistently make me feel like they like me and are interested in what I have to say are head-nodders. It takes a little practice to start being a good head-nodder, but it's worth the effort.

Therefore, if you want people to think that you are interested in what they have to say and that you are not defensive about it, be an open-armed, open-legged, forward-leaning head-nodder.

Of course other gestures carry meanings too, such as the well-known gesture that angry kids occasionally give us or each other, but those aren't used as constantly as the ones that I have just mentioned.

When you read the title of this chapter, you may not have thought about the messages that are sent nonverbally, but you undoubtedly thought about the messages that you send verbally. Let's talk about ways that we say the things we say, and then we will talk about how to more skillfully phrase the things that we say.

One of the things that Don did that made Sherilyn feel awkward is use formal speech instead of informal. Formal speech is careful, precise, and complex. Informal speech is relaxed, imprecise, and simple.

For example, I could say, "To whom do you wish to speak?" and give a very different impression than if I said, "Who ya lookin' for?" The words themselves mean the same thing, but the formality or informality of the words carries a very different message.

I watched Sherilyn when she told Don that half of the kids in their cottage wanted to go to the mall on Friday night, and that the other half wanted to go to the high school football game.

"What is it that you want to do about it?" he crisply asked. He would have gleaned the same information if he had casually said, "Which do ya think we oughta do?" and made Sherilyn feel comfortable. He used a formal style of speech to make her feel uncomfortable, although she couldn't have said why she felt that way.

Another way that Don distanced himself from Sherilyn in that comment was his use of pronouns. When we want to make someone feel in close unity with us, we use the words "we" and "us." When we want to make them feel more distant and apart from us, we use the words "you" and "I." By not saying, "Which do ya think *we* oughta do?" Don sent the clear message, "You and I may work in the same cottage, but don't get the idea that that means that you and I are a team." If he had said, "Which do ya think we oughta do?" his use of the word *we* would have carried the message, "We are a team."

Another way that we phrase our messages that carries either unity or disunity is referred to as *speech convergence* or *speech divergence*. Speech convergence means making your speech more like that of your conversational partner. Speech divergence means making your speech less like that of your conversational partner.

For example, when I am with my cowboy friends who say, "She don't" and "He don't," I say, "She don't" and "He don't." But when I am with my college professor friends, I say, "He doesn't," and "She doesn't." I converge my speech style to be like that of whichever group I am talking to, so that I show my unity with them.

In the same way, when I want to show someone that I don't like them, or that I am really ticked off, I diverge my speech pattern from theirs and move from an informal to a very formal speech style.

A really overt example of the use of speech convergence and divergence sometimes occurs when we walk into a room in which several of our kids are talking. As we enter, they are talking a mild case of teenagerese, but when they notice us, they lapse into ultra teenagerese. The message that they are sending us is this: *We are us, and we are insiders to each other. You are definitely not part of us; we don't even talk like you do. Go away.*

Kids who are bilingual may even lapse into their other language when you enter the room. The intent is not so much that they are talking about something that you aren't supposed to know about, but rather that they are showing group solidarity and reminding you that you are an outsider.

People who are close often develop their own personal language to demonstrate the intimacy of their relationship. My husband, Kelvin, and I have a language that we have developed over the years. That language was really powerful in helping create a bond between us and our boys when we were houseparents. For example, we called the boys "Bear Cubs," and they soon began referring to themselves as Bear Cubs. We called food "grubs and berries," and soon the boys were referring to eating their grubs and berries. (Note that these were teenage boys, not little boys, which made it especially surprising to me.)

This worked so well for us that the boys from other cottages began making fun of our boys and began using the term Bear Cubs as a put-down, much in the way that they also used the term "homo" at that time. This was brought about by the boys from other cottages feeling like outsiders when our boys talked to each other and to us. Everyone resents feeling like an outsider, and since anything which focused on the members of our cottage being insiders, those who were not part of our cadre resented it.

If I was surprised by the other kids resenting the closeness that our Bear Cub language represented, I was blown away by several of the other houseparents feeling jealous of our close relationships as well. The boys would report to us how the houseparents of this cottage or that would use the term "Bear Cubs" as a put-down. I was flabbergasted that houseparents wouldn't applaud anything that helped a cottage family feel close. But they didn't applaud. They actively worked to destroy that closeness for the same reason that the boys in their cottages did: they subconsciously felt left out and resented it.

The use of the term Bear Cubs brings us to another way that people communicate to show closeness, and that is by using nicknames. When someone gives us a nickname, we feel like they have singled us out as being special. Even if everyone in the cottage has a nickname, each person still feels singled out and special because of it. The boys in our cottage prized their individual nicknames, and some of them even went so far as to start signing their school papers "Little Joe" or "Big John" or "Ace." Their nicknames made them feel special, in the same way that when your spouse calls you by the special nicknames you share, you feel special.

The most important thing that I can tell you about communication is to communicate with what the famous psychologist, Carl Rogers, called *empathy*. Communicating with empathy means listening to what the other person says by trying to feel what she's feeling. Try to get inside her head and her heart and think what she is thinking and feel what she is feeling. Rogers said it better than I ever could.

> The way of being with another person which is termed empathic has several facets. It means entering the private perceptual world of the other and becoming thoroughly at home in it. It involves being sensitive, moment to moment, to the changing felt meanings which flow in this other person, to the fear or rage or tenderness or confusion or whatever, that he/she is experiencing. It means temporarily living in his/her life, moving about in it delicately without making judgements.... It includes communicating your sensings of his/her world as you look with fresh and unfrightened eyes at elements of which the individual is fearful. It means frequently checking with him/her as to the accuracy of your sensings, and being guided by the responses you receive. You are a confident companion to the other in his/her world....

> To be with another in this way means that for the time being you lay aside the views and values you hold for yourself in order to enter another's world without prejudice....
>
> ... being empathic is a complex, demanding, strong yet subtle and gentle way of being. (p. 4)

To be empathic includes actively trying to figure out what the other person *means* by what she says, not simply taking at face value that what she means is what you *think* that she means. When we communicate with someone, we take for granted that they mean what we think they mean. That's often not the case. This happens especially often when we communicate with persons of the opposite sex, or with persons of a different generation. Leah, a housemother, gave me a wonderful example.

> When Peter and Lori moved in as our assistant houseparents, I was really relieved. We'd been working shorthanded for two months, and Tom and I were exhausted. Well, I was determined that this time nothing was going to go wrong, and we were going to be able to keep Peter and Lori around. It was easy to become friends with Lori, she was ready for a friend.... And it was easy to become friends with Peter, too. Or so I thought.... (Looks off into the distance.) Then I realized that what I meant as friendly overtures, Peter thought was me coming on to him. (Furrows brow.) When I'd tell him on Sunday mornings how handsome he looked, or when I would tell him how great it was to have him around to help with the kids when Tom was doing other stuff, I meant it to be friendly.... Then one day when Lori was on a doctor run and Tom was picking up some supplies at the hardware store, Peter came to the laundry room where I was doing clothes.... I'll never forget it.... I was folding a sheet, and he reached out and put his hand over mine! Then he said, "I thought we'd never get the chance to be alone." I told him that I didn't feel that way about him, and he looked crushed. He asked me why I kept telling him how great he looked and stuff like that, and I realized that he thought I'd been coming on to him.... Well, it was never the same after that.... He and Lori didn't have to wait long before they got their own house, and I was glad.... Of course, then we had to break in a whole new set of houseparents....

Like Peter, a whole heck of a lot of the time we think other people mean something by what they say that they don't mean at all. When Leah told Peter that he looked handsome and that she was glad he was living in their house, what she meant was, "I want you to feel at home and to stay a long time." What he thought she meant was, "I want your bod!" A classic case of miscommunication.

If Peter had practiced empathy, or what Carl Rogers called *empathic listening*, he would have tried to have gotten into Lori's head in order to figure out what she was meaning.

When Rogers says that we must check with our conversation partner frequently about her meanings, what he means is that we must paraphrase what we think she is meaning and give her the chance to confirm or deny it. Take for example a miscommunication between Carmen and Lisa.

> Carmen says: "I'm so tired. The work around here never gets finished." Carmen means: *It's hard being a housemom.*
> Lisa hears what Carmen says. Lisa thinks: *Carmen means that I'm not doing my share of the work.* Lisa gets mad.

If Lisa had checked out what Carmen meant, she would have said, "Do you think that I'm not doing my share of the work?"

Then Carmen could have said, "No way! We both work our tails off. What I meant was that being a housemom is hard work."

If we check to make sure that what we *think* the other person means is *actually* what he means, then we can avoid problems. Take the example of Tawney and Lorinda. Lorinda told me the following story.

> Tawney always (prepared) the after-school snacks. She's really into baking and likes to make the kids individually decorated cupcakes, and stuff like that. Well, she asked me to do the kids' snacks after school, because she wasn't going to get back from the dentist with (a resident) in time.... Well, I'm not into baking, so I just put out some oranges and apples.... (Shrugs.) She gets home and she's all pissed off. I don't know what's wrong, and it turns out that she thought that because I didn't bake something that I lied to her about saying I'd do the snacks.... She didn't think that fruit was a snack, because the kids know that they can always have a piece of fruit.... But to me, fruit is still a snack, even if the kids can have it any time....

When Tawney asked Lorinda to make the snacks, Lorinda could have asked for clarification by asking, "Is there something specific that you want me to fix?" But since Lorinda didn't ask Tawney to clarify herself, Tawney assumed that Lorinda was agreeing to *bake* after-school snacks and then felt that Lorinda had been lying because she didn't bake the kids' snacks.

So empathic listening involves trying to get inside the other person's head and heart, think what she is thinking, and feel what she is feeling, and two ways of doing that are paraphrasing what you think her meaning is and asking her to clarify her meaning. While doing both of these, it is important to concentrate on what are the other person's *meanings* of words. What does she mean? To Tawney, the meaning of the word *snack* is baked goods. To Lorinda, the meaning of the word snack is anything that is eaten between meals. They used the same word but had very different meanings.

Let me give one more example.

Lorinda's husband, Stu, was really crazy about his dog, Cappy. Stu and Lorinda were going to the funeral of Lorinda's favorite aunt and were going to be gone for three days. They were going to fly, because it was too long a trip to make by car in the time allotted. Stu asked Tawney's husband, Bill, to take care of the dog.

> (Bill) told me not to worry, that he'd take care of everything, so I felt good about it.... Then the night we got home, it was about two (o'clock) in the morning, raining like crazy, and here I found Cappy huddled by the back door, sopping wet. Storms scare him, and we always bring him in the house when it rains. Bill should have put (the dog) inside when it started storming. I'll never trust (Bill) again, and I told him so.

I got Bill's side of the story.

> I hate it that (Stu) is pissed, but when he said would I take care of his dog, to me that meant would I feed it and water it, and I did. Hell, I never thought about putting (the dog) in the house when it stormed. The dog has a doghouse. It should have gone in there. Why didn't (the dog) just go in the doghouse? If Stu had *told* me to put the dog inside if it stormed, I would have....

Bill and Stu had very different ideas about the meaning of *take care of the dog*, and their assumption that each knew what the other meant by taking care of the dog caused a bitter misunderstanding.

One way that meanings may be misunderstood is if the conversation partners have different communication styles. There are three different categories of communication styles: *direct vs. indirect, elaborate vs. succinct,* and *instrumental vs. affective.* Once you identify your styles and those of your partners, then you can keep that in mind as you try and listen empathically. You might learn, for example, that when John says he feels "a little rough this morning," that because his is a succinct style of communication, what he actually means is that he has a temperature of 103 degrees and needs to stay in bed. Let's take a look at the three categories.

The first category is direct vs. indirect. In general, Americans use a direct style of communication. I say in general, because, compared to other countries, Americans are very direct. But within the American culture, there can be a wide range of variation. Direct vs. indirect refers to how explicitly you express your true needs, wants, and feelings. Bob uses a direct style when he says, "I feel like hell today and I've got to stay in bed." John uses an indirect style when he says that he feels "a little rough this morning." Direct-style people often think that indirect-style people are wishy-washy, while indirect-style people often think that direct-style people are rude and obnoxious.

Sherrie, an assistant housemom, was an indirect-style communicator. She told me this about Helen, the direct-style senior housemom in her home.

> I hate to do doctor runs, but Helen always assigns me to do them. I'd much rather stay home and do the laundry.... But when she asks me what I'd rather do, I tell her "do the laundry" and she sends me on the doctor runs anyway.... (Shrugs.)

Helen told me her side of the story when I told her how the younger woman felt.

> I never dreamed that she didn't like to do doctor runs! I thought I was doing her a favor by letting her get out of the house.... I'd ask her, "Do you wanna do the runs or the laundry?" She'd say, "Whatever you want me to. I don't mind doing the laundry." She didn't say, "Hell no, I don't want to go to town," so I thought she was just being nice to offer to do the laundry ... being a good kid, you know.... All she had to do was tell me. I'da done the runs. Laundry's a pain. I'd much rather sit in a doctor's office and read a magazine than stay here and wash some kid's dirty undershorts.

Once Helen and Sherrie each understood how the other communicated, Sherrie became much happier with their relationship. She learned to be a little more direct, and Helen learned to listen more sensitively.

Direct vs. indirect style often enters into opposite sex communication problems. In general, men tend to be more direct style than women do. This helps explain why women sometimes say, "My husband never listens to me." What is happening is that the woman is communicating indirectly, and her husband doesn't understand what she means, because he listens with a direct style. Todd told me this about his wife, Twyla.

> Yesterday I was reading the paper, and Twyla's vacuuming. Then she tells me that she's really tired and doesn't think she can get all her work done, and I say, "Sorry, Honey," and the next thing I know, she's mad.

Twyla's version of the story was like this.

> I'm always asking Todd to help me, but he won't do it. He never even listens when I tell him that I feel like he's not carrying his share of the load... Yesterday I was vacuuming, and what was he doing? Reading the paper, so I asked him to help me. What did he do? Said sorry, and kept on reading his paper.

When Twyla was trying to tell Todd in her indirect way that he should help her, he thought that she was just passing the time of day. She, on the other hand, thought that he was ignoring her needs. Sound familiar?

The elaborate vs. succinct style, like the other styles, can be thought of as a continuum. On one end is the elaborate style. On the other end is the succinct style. And in the middle is the exacting style. This communication dimension refers to the amount and kind of speech a person uses.

The elaborate communicator uses rich, flowery phrases in everyday speech. She likes metaphors and has the heart of a poet. A wonderful example of elaborate communicators are people from the Arabic countries. Whereas an American man might say to his wife, "You look nice," an Arabic man might say, "You are the bloom of a thousand roses! Your smile shines like the brilliance of the sun and melts my heart into a puddle at your feet." Makes the American husband look pretty pitiful, if you ask me.

Harry and Frank were housedads who were fond of each other. Frank was an elaborate style communicator, and Harry had learned to deal with that. He said, "I just use the Twenty-Five Percent Rule when I listen to Frank. Then I know what he means."

I had never heard of the Twenty-Five Percent Rule, so I asked Harry what he meant.

"Well, Frank exaggerates everything. If he has to make three trips into town, he says he made four. If he was so hungry that he ate six hotdogs, he says he had eight. If he says that he didn't get to sleep until two a.m., I figure he got to sleep at midnight. I just take everything he says, reduce it by 25%, and know that that's what he means."

Harry had learned the art of empathic listening. He learned to think the way Frank thinks and feel the way Frank feels when they communicated and that made for a successful relationship between them.

The person who uses the exacting speech style says neither more nor less than is required. While the exacting communicator will tell us exactly what he needs, thinks, or wants, he may come across as sterile and colorless. "He's the most boring man in the world," a young housemother told me of the senior housefather in her house. "Talking to him is like talking to a computer."

The succinct style is typified by the notion of the Vermont farmer. It reminds me of an old story. It seems that a fellow from the south was traveling through Vermont. It was a foggy day, and since he wasn't sure where he was, he was relieved to see a farmer tightening up a strand of fence. "Hey mister," called the traveler pointing ahead, "is that the way to the next town?"

"Yeah," said the farmer, so the southerner thanked him and headed off down the road and fell into the river where the bridge had washed out.

The southerner dragged himself out of the river and trudged back to the farmer's house. "The bridge is out!" he said to the Vermonter.

"Yeah," said the farmer.

The southerner was flabbergasted. "You mean that you knew the bridge was out?"

"Yeah," said the farmer.

The traveler's eyes bugged out. "Then why didn't you tell me?"

"Yuh didn't ask," said the farmer.

People who use succinct style use understatement, pauses, and silence in their conversations. The listener has to work hard in order to understand the message of the succinct style communicator.

Instrumental vs. affective communication style refers to one's orientation to get right to the business at hand, or to take one's time and build a relationship with the other person. It can be thought of as a product vs. process orientation. The instrumental communicator can be thought of as the American businessman: fly in Friday morning, strike a deal, get out, and go home Friday night. The affective communicator can be thought of as the Latin American businessman. He tells you to come a week early. He wants you to spend the week dining, drinking, and sunning together on the beach. He wants you to get to know each other, become friends, talk about your families. Then, if everything feels right and the proper bonds have been forged, you can talk business. Doesn't that explain a lot about the difficulties of forging international business deals with our neighbors to the south? What American businessmen see as wasting time, Latin American businessmen see as the most important part of doing business. What American businessmen see as doing business, Latin American businessmen see as rudeness.

In this chapter, we have talked about communication and how to improve your communication skills by being empathic. We've talked about paraphrasing and asking for clarification and about communication styles. We hope that by using these skills, you can head off problems before they start. But if problems do start, either between yourself and others, or between kids, then you have to use conflict resolution techniques. That is what we will cover in the next chapter.

Chapter 14

RESOLVING CONFLICT FOR KIDS AND CO-WORKERS

In the last chapter, we discussed communication skills. In this chapter, we want to talk about conflict resolution skills. First we will discuss the nature and value of conflict. Then, we'll talk about styles of resolving conflict. Win-win conflict resolution and the role of a third person in resolving conflict will then be discussed.

Whenever I have said the word *conflict* and asked people to respond to it, people have responded with words such as fight, hit, war, yell, anger. Those are generally considered to be negative words. However, experts in conflict resolution say that conflict should be seen as a positive thing. They say that conflict is a natural part of life and that it can be an opportunity for growth, both for an individual and for a relationship. I've read that the Chinese symbol for conflict is a combination of the symbol for danger and for that of opportunity. Try to stress the idea of opportunity when you think about conflict.

People learn a style of conflict resolution which they tend to use most frequently as they grow up. They learn this style from their brothers and sisters, from other kids, from their caregivers, TV, and so on. The lessons kids learn about conflict as they are growing influence the way they feel, think and behave when faced with conflict as adults in their work, in their community, in their home, and in their friendships. For example, the Rambo movies that have been extremely popular among kids and adults illustrate violence as the way to resolve conflict and teach kids to use violence to solve their own conflicts.

There are basically three ways of resolving conflict: fight, flight, or problem solving. Fighting is what most people think of when they think about conflict. Fighting and verbal aggression seem to come naturally to kids, and it certainly makes for exciting movies or TV. However, as we look at the problem of violence in the world today, it's obvious that we need to teach better ways of dealing with conflict.

There are times when avoiding conflict is really the best way to go. After all, it's been said that discretion is the better part of valor, and sometimes the discreet thing to do is get the heck out of the way. If another person is out of control, then avoiding him may be the most reasonable solution for the time being, although it's apt to be a temporary solution. For example, ten-year-old Billy Watson lost control of his temper. He was swinging a baseball bat and threatening to hit his cottagemate, SueAnne Costanegra. For the moment, SueAnne's best option was to get away. She did, and Billy ended up hitting the bat against the tree (instead of SueAnne) until his anger dissipated.

If Billy and SueAnne are going to continue to live in the same cottage, then they're going to have a continuing relationship, and neither Billy's aggression nor SueAnne's running away are effective means of dealing with problems. These kids are going to have conflict over time, and if he's going to continue aggressing, and she's going to continue running away, then both of them are learning poor conflict resolution skills.

If, as an adult, Billy hits people whenever he's angry, he will not be able to keep a job, a friend, or a marriage partner. Billy's a prime candidate for dancing the jailhouse rock. On the other hand, if SueAnne always runs away in the face of anger, then she'll find people running over her at work, home, and in her neighborhood. Even worse, if they have each learned this fight-flight pattern for resolving conflict, then Billy and SueAnne may each look for a marriage partner who will play the game they've learned so well. After all, that will seem normal to them. That may be why the cycle of domestic violence is so difficult to end.

Fight and flight are complementary in that they fit together like two pieces of a puzzle. However, with fight and flight solutions to conflict, there is at best one winner and one loser. That's what we call a win-lose situation. In some sense, maybe everybody loses, including Billy, who gets his way and appears to win. If SueAnne runs away, then even though Billy has the bat, there's no one to pitch a ball to him. That's what is called a lose-lose situation. The question is: how can Billy and SueAnne, or you and I, resolve conflict in a way that everyone wins, or in what we call a win-win situation?

It may not be possible for everyone to get what they think they *want* in every conflict situation. But people *can* get what they *need* without depriving others of their needs. So Billy wants to continue to bat and SueAnne doesn't want to pitch all the time. She wants to bat sometimes.

But with a fight 'n' fight solution, nobody gets to bat. If we look at what Billy and SueAnne really need from their game, we find the following: They need to have fun, and they need to have a feeling of belonging (friends 'n' family), and they need to feel competent.

The freedom in this case is for the kids to have some choice about what they do and how they do it. In other words, they choose to play the game and they can make up their own rules. So the basic question we have to look at in helping them resolve their conflict is not just what they want (to bat) but what they need. If we can help Billy and SueAnne identify what they really need, then they can together figure out ways to meet their needs while getting most, or at least some, of what they want.

The place where most people get stuck in conflict is when they attempt to bargain over position rather than needs. Billy's position was that he was going to continue to bat. SueAnne's position was that she wanted to bat. As long as Billy and SueAnne center on their positions, there's not apt to be a solution to their problem that is satisfying to both of them.

Take for example junior housedad Don Woo and his senior counterpart, Barry Newton. They got into an argument about who, if anyone, should be allowed to watch "NYPD Blue." (For those of you who don't know, "NYPD Blue" is a TV program that's been criticized because of excessive violence and nudity.)

Barry said, "Any of the boys who are old enough to have ten-thirty bedtimes instead of nine o'clock bedtimes are old enough to watch."

Don disagreed. "Look," he said. "I don't care whether the kids are over or under fifteen. That stuff doesn't have any place in our cottage."

"It's better for the kids to watch it here with us where can talk about it than to see it somewhere else. All you gotta do to get a kid to be determined to do something is make it forbidden in the cottage."

Don said, "If we let 'em watch it here, it's like we are telling them that it's okay to be violent and promiscuous, and it's not."

Barry and Don can remain locked in an argument on that question forever, or Barry can say, "I'm in charge and here's what we're gonna do." Don can either give in to Barry's authority, continue to argue, or quit his job. A solution won't come until they look at each man's need or interest behind his position and work on ways to meet the need of each as reflected in the TV-watching question.

Sometimes people don't resolve conflicts effectively because they don't have the skills. Sometimes they don't solve conflicts effectively because of an imbalance in power. If one is much stronger physically or mentally, or if one is in a position of power over the other, then the strong can dominate. This results in a forced solution rather than an ideal solution.

When people don't have the skills to resolve conflicts by themselves, or they don't have the ability to balance the power themselves, it is often helpful for a skilled third person to help them resolve their conflict. This happens in the courts when a judge and jury hear both sides and render a decision. Sometimes someone called an *arbitrator* is employed to do the same thing. In both of these cases, however, the parties involved in the conflict give up the control over the outcome of the conflict. Once the arbitrator, judge, or jury hears all of the evidence presented by both sides, then the people who have the conflict have no further control over the outcome. They may both end up unhappy and with their needs unmet.

This happens all the time with children and adults. Monica and Heather got into an argument about which radio station to listen to. Monica was a country western fan, and Heather thought of herself as a rocker. Unfortunately, they had to room together.

After dinner one night, they got into a shouting and shoving match over the radio. Their housemom, Maria Castenada, heard them and she came in to settle things. "Okay," she said, hands on her hips, "just turn the radio off."

As a result, everyone was unhappy and felt bad, including Maria. Their argument was over, but what did Monica and Heather learn and what will happen the next time they disagree about the radio or anything else?

There is another way that Maria could have helped the roomies settle their problem. She could have taken the role of what is called a *mediator*. A mediator is a third party who doesn't take sides and doesn't make decisions for people. Instead, the mediator helps people to make their *own* decisions in ways that protect everyone's needs.

In order to be a good mediator, you need to be a good listener, not take sides, and let people settle their own disputes. Remember in the last chapter that we talked about eye contact, body position, and distance as ways of helping people to talk. We also talked about the importance of paraphrasing as a way of helping people know that we understand them. When you paraphrase someone's words, you also help her to clarify and understand her own thoughts and feelings.

For example, Freeman Lee came home and slammed his books down on the table. He flopped down in a chair and stuffed a whole piece of chocolate cake in his mouth at once. His housemom, Cathy Baretta, noticed how upset he was. She stopped pouring milk, came over and sat down next to him.

"Have a hard day?" she asked.

Freeman swallowed his mouthful of cake. "That damn old math teacher pissed me off!" he said.

Cathy paraphrased Freeman's words. "You're really angry about what happened in math class."

Freeman nodded his head and his eyes teared. He said, "The old bitch accused me of copying my homework, and I didn't!"

Cathy paraphrased again. "It sounds like your feelings were *really* hurt when she said that."

"Yeah. Well, you know I really hadn't been trying on my homework. Then last night after you and me talked about it, I decided to do a really good job, just to show everyone what I could do. You know! You saw the paper when I got finished. Then when I turned it in today, she said, 'You couldn't have done this work by yourself, Freeman. Who'd you copy off of?' She said it in front of everybody!"

Again Cathy paraphrased. "So after our talk, you decided to turn over a new leaf and do good in school. And you got put down anyway."

Freeman nodded. "Yeah. No sense in me even trying in school."

Another paraphrase from Cathy: "Sometimes you just feel like giving up."

By paraphrasing, both Cathy and Freeman came to understand that he wasn't just angry, or not even just embarrassed, but that he was so discouraged that he felt like giving up on being successful in school.

In the process of mediation, we begin by listening and paraphrasing to help the person express and clarify her thoughts and feelings. We do that in the presence of the person she's having conflict with as a way of helping the other person to understand her. We're also teaching both parties how to express their needs and how to listen to each other.

In addition to listening as a way of helping people to express their thoughts and feelings, we need to teach the skill to them directly. Perhaps the best approach to teaching self-expression is using what are called *I-messages*. There are three basic parts to an I-message: (1) what happened, (2) how I felt when it happened, and (3) why I felt that way.

Take for example, Elaine, whose houseparents had taught her how to make I-messages. Elaine's best friend and cottage roomie, Anita, sat across the classroom from Elaine in science. Next to Anita sat Sherilyn, a new girl in town. One morning when the science teacher had the kids working in pairs, Elaine looked up and saw Anita and Sherilyn looking at her and laughing. After class, Elaine walked up to Anita and said, "When you and Sherilyn looked at me and laughed, my feelings were hurt because I thought my best friend was laughing at me."

"Good grief, no, girlfriend!" said Anita. "We wasn't laughin' at you! I was braggin' to Sherilyn about how you set them boys at the mall straight when they tried to hit on us! She thought it was just too cool!"

If Elaine had not known how to use I-messages when her feelings were hurt, she might have handled it like a Sherita, a girl not trained in I-messages, handled a similar situation. When Sherita incorrectly thought that her best friend, Jerice, was gossipping to a classmate about her, Sherita attacked her after class.

"You bitch!" she screeched. "I hate you! Who do you think you are, gossipping about me! I showed you! I just told Aaron Babbitt that you were sleeping with half the boys in the cottage!"

In the first case, an I-message solved a problem and saved a friendship. In the second case, poor communication cost a friendship. Notice, too, that in the first case, Elaine puts the emphasis on herself and takes ownership of her feelings. In contrast, in the second case, Sherita used a You-message and made the conflict worse, which screwed everything up.

The problem was solved through a message of *what I feel,* instead of aggravated by a message of *what you did,* so that in an I-message, you give the other person information about their behavior and your feelings. They then have the responsibility of deciding what to do with that information and are not put in a position of defending themselves from a personal attack.

To teach people how to make I-messages, we start with a three-step structured format:

1. I felt _____,
2. when you _____,
3. because _____.

As people become comfortable with the process of using I-messages, they drop the formal structure and begin to give the same information in a way that is natural to them.

Rosemary Cleeman was a warm, bubbly housemom, but like many folks, getting places on time wasn't her strong suit. She was hired to work in a cottage with Celina Winthorst. Celina was a well-organized housemom and very punctual. On several occasions, Celina had been annoyed when Rosemary was late returning with the van from a run to town.

One afternoon, when Celina was scheduled to take the van to deliver one of the girls to a dentist appointment, she had to wait fifteen minutes before Rosemary returned with the vehicle.

"You're late again," Celina said. "You make me so mad because you are totally irresponsible! You're the worst houseparent I've ever had to work with!"

Rosemary then responded, "Well, I had to talk with (one of the residents) and that was more important! If you were caring at all to the girls, you would have known that she was upset this morning, and you would have talked to her about it! But you don't ever have time to help the girls, you're so balled up with your damn schedules!"

Thus we have the beginning of a world-class fight between two housemoms instead of a solution to a problem or conflict. If, when Celina first became irritated because her schedule was disrupted by Rosemary, she had used an I-message (I feel really anxious when you are late because my motto is, "Plan your work and work your plan") instead of the You-message that she used, then they could have resolved the problem before nuclear war broke out.

Here are a couple of real-life situations for you to practice I-messages.

> Vickie Masterson sent eight-year-old Buzz to his room until supper for not cleaning up his bathroom vanity before he left for school that morning. Fred Dawson, the junior housedad, came by and saw Buzz sitting in his room. When Buzz told him what had happened, Fred asked Buzz if he had now cleaned the vanity and learned his lesson. Buzz said that he had and he did. Fred told Buzz that he could come out of his room, but to be sure not to repeat the infraction. When Vickie found out about Fred's giving Buzz a break, she was upset and said to Fred,
> "I feel _____,
> when you _____,
> because _____."

Did you feel comfortable making an I-message for Vickie? Try one more:

> Royce Alan was a sixth grader whose cottage chore was to take out the trash. For the last three days, his housedad, Peter Vetnovitch,

had to remind him three or four times before he did his chore. Finally, Peter decided to try an I-message. He said to Royce Alan, "I feel _____, when you _____, because _____."

Note that the order of the first two parts of an I-message can be switched if that's more comfortable for you.

You now know how to do active listening and make I-messages. So, let's go on and outline the rules and procedures for mediating conflict resolution.

The rules are short and sweet.

Rules

1. No fighting.
2. No putdowns or namecalling.
3. No interruptions.
4. Listen when someone else is talking.
5. At first, disputants talk through the mediator.
6. Try to solve the problem.

That didn't take long, did it? Now for the procedures of mediation.

Procedures

If the disputants are still really upset, then it's a good idea for you as the mediator to meet with them separately. At this time, go over the process of mediation and get them to agree to the rules. Also at this point, you should make sure that the disputants are there voluntarily and that they understand that this is not going to exempt them from house consequences for rule infractions. In other words, you don't want them to come to mediation in order to escape the consequences of their behavior.

For example, the cottage punishment for stealing a CD is staying in your room after school for a week. Billy Joe stole Rita's Garth Brooks CD, sold it to a kid at school, and used the money to go to the movie on town night. The CD is gone and so is the money. Although Billy Joe is required to stay in his room for a week as punishment, you, as the houseparent, could mediate the dispute between Billy Joe and Rita over the stolen CD so that they could resolve the problem that now has come between them.

In meeting with each child individually, you explain that your role is to help *them* solve *their* problem. Make sure that the kids understand that your role is not to solve the problem for them.

Explain that you will not take sides, even if you have an opinion. Also, promise to keep confidential whatever is said in the mediation process. You should tell the disputants about any exceptions to your confidentiality, such as illegal behavior, abuse, or intent to harm self or others.

Some mediators think that it's important to have the disputants sign a written agreement at the end of the mediation process. If you plan to do this, this is a good time to make that known.

Let's pretend that you are mediating for Billy Joe and Rita.

Once the individual meetings are over, bring both disputants into the room and have one sit on your right and the other on your left. Although they are facing in the general direction of each other, it's good to have them at an angle, because that is less threatening nonverbal behavior than directly facing each other.

Talking to each in turn, read each rule and ask, "Will you agree to follow this rule?" That way each disputant understands that the other is also agreeing to follow each rule.

Then turning to either the disputant who asked for the mediation, or the one who is most upset, ask her, "Tell us what happened from your point of view and how do you feel about it?" (Avoid asking them to tell "their side" of the story. Saying "your side" implies that there is a right and wrong side. Instead, we want to stress that there are two points of view of the same circumstance.)

Using your listening skills, paraphrase the thoughts and feelings of Person #1, in this case, Rita. Ask her if she'd like to correct or add to your feedback. Continue listening until that person seems satisfied that she has been heard and understood by you.

Next, turn to Person #2 (Billy Joe) and repeat the process. Once he is satisfied that he has been heard and understood by you, then turn back to the first disputant and ask her to paraphrase what Billy Joe said happened from his point of view and how Billy Joe felt about it.

You may need to point out that Rita doesn't need to agree with Billy Joe's point of view, but that it is important for her to be accurate about Billy Joe's thoughts and feelings. Then ask Billy Joe if Rita was correct in her understanding. If not, Billy Joe restates and Rita paraphrases Billy

Joe's restatements until he is satisfied that Rita understands his point of view and feelings.

Then ask Billy Joe to do the same for Rita, by paraphrasing what Rita said happened from her point of view and how Rita felt about it. Ask Rita if Billy Joe paraphrased her correctly. If not, Rita continues restating and Billy Joe continues paraphrasing until Rita is satisfied that she has been understood.

Your paraphrasing of each person's thoughts and feelings not only helps each to clarify what happened from her or his point of view but serves as a model for each to understand the other.

Now, turn to Rita and ask her what she needs in order to resolve her problem. If she states a position, use paraphrasing to reframe her statement into what she *needs* to resolve her problem. Repeat the process with the other disputant (Billy Joe), asking him what he needs in order to solve his problem. Then ask each disputant to restate what the other needs in order to resolve his or her problem until both are satisfied that the other knows what he or she needs in order to solve the problem.

Once everyone is satisfied that the problem is understood from their point of view and has had an opportunity to express their needs, you're ready to begin looking for a solution. The technique used for finding a solution is called *brainstorming*.

In brainstorming, there are only two rules. First, everyone mentions every idea that they can think of related to the problem and the mediator writes them down. Second, no one criticizes any idea. This means that everyone has to understand that suggesting an idea is *not* the same as agreeing to an idea. The intent is to get as many possibilities on the table as you can. The reason we don't critique the ideas as they are proposed is that tends to stop the flow of ideas. Once you seem to have run out of ideas, then you begin evaluating them.

Here are the ideas that Billy Joe and Rita came up with during their brainstorming session:

> BJ and R tell manager of CD's R US that the CD was damaged when R bought it and try to get a new one for free.
> BJ steals a CD and gives it to R.
> BJ gives R three of his CD's of his choosing.
> BJ gives R five of his CD's of her choosing.
> BJ buys R a new Garth Brooks CD.
> BJ does R's cottage chores for two weeks.

> BJ has to go to school naked.
> The theater owner has to give R a free pass.
> Everybody in the cottage gives R $1.50 so she can buy a new CD.
> BJ has to pay R $15 today.

The mediator's job at this point is to insure fairness and balance to the problem solution. You should also be sure that any solution agreed upon is actually do-able by the disputants. Remember, a person can only control his own behavior and not anyone else's. Therefore, the solution must be something that the disputants themselves can actually do. It has to be realistic. It has to be specific. And you have to agree on when, where, and how it will be accomplished.

For example, Billy Joe and Rita can't agree that the movie owner will give Rita a free pass to compensate for the loss of her CD, since the kids can't control the theater owner's behavior. On the other hand, if the CD is worth $15 and Billy Joe has no money, they can't agree that he will immediately give Rita the $15.

What you would need to do, in that case, is to help Billy Joe look at his income and set a timetable for repayment that is reasonable and do-able for him. On the other hand, if Rita demands immediate compensation and Billy Joe has no money, she will have to agree to some non-monetary compensation, such as that he will do her chores for a week or he will give her some of his CD's.

Billy Joe and Rita finally agreed on the following:

> Billy Joe will do extra chores for money for the next three weeks. He will give Rita $5 each Saturday evening. At the end of three weeks, Billy Joe and Rita will go to CD's R US and buy Rita a new Garth Brooks CD. Then, Rita will tell her friends that Billy Joe has replaced her CD. Billy Joe will apologize for stealing the CD and Rita will accept his apology.

Note that although an apology is frequently part of the written agreement, or just occurs spontaneously, you as the mediator should *not* urge or require an apology. A forced apology doesn't mean a damn thing to anyone.

The next step consists of writing AND SIGNING the agreement. You should sign as a witness and the agreement should be dated.

The final step is to decide what the disputants will tell their friends. A common agreement is to simply tell friends, "We have resolved our problem," or "We've solved our problem." You may think that your kids can't keep their mouths shut and only respond with "We've solved our problem," without going into all the details, but surprisingly enough, even gang members have kept the promise to just say, "We've solved our problem," and nothing more. The secret is to have the kids decide what they are really willing and able to do.

I then usually congratulate the disputants for solving their problem. It's an important step, because using this approach is scary and a lot of hard work. It's important for the kids to know that an adult recognizes how hard and risky it was for them to agree to mediation. The congratulations symbolize the approval of using a non-violent and productive way of solving problems.

If you use this process with the kids in your cottage, they will learn through experience how to listen to each other better and how to express their thoughts and feelings to each other better.

If you have a kid in your cottage who seems to have a feel for the process and is interested, you may want to have her co-mediate with you and eventually become a cottage mediator. It is important that this individual have the following characteristics: be able to stay neutral, be respected by the other kids, be a good listener, and be mature enough to keep confidentiality of the disputants she mediates.

This peer-mediation process has been used by student mediators in many schools with startling success. The ability to resolve your own disputes, to listen to others, to express yourself, and to help other people resolve disputes is a life skill highly desired by business and industry. In the process of helping your kids resolve day-to-day problems, you can teach them a skill that they will use for the rest of their life and that will significantly improve the quality of their life. Kids that learn this skill will use it a thousand times more often than they will ever use algebra or geometry. (That comes from an old algebra and geometry teacher.)

On the next page, the rules and procedures for conflict mediation are briefly outlined. If you are going to try mediation with your kids or for other houseparents who are involved in a dispute, you are welcome to photocopy the page and take it with you to the mediation for quick reference.

In this chapter, we have discussed conflict resolution and mediation. We have included rules and procedures for mediation and are closing with a quick checklist for you to use. In the next chapter, we will present hints for houseparents given to us by houseparents themselves on a national survey we conducted.

Copy this page to take with you when you mediate.

Rules

1. No fighting.
2. No put-downs or name-calling.
3. No interruptions.
4. Listen when someone else is talking.
5. At first, disputants talk through the mediator.
6. Try to solve the problem.

Procedures

1. First, hold a separate meeting with each disputant. (Agree to mediate and follow the rules.)
2. Then, hold the meeting with both disputants.
3. In the other disputant's presence, each disputant agrees to follow each rule.
4. Invite one disputant to tell what happened from her point of view and how she felt about what happened.
5. You paraphrase what she said.
6. The other disputant tells what happened from his point of view and how he felt about what happened.
7. You paraphrase what he said.
8. Once each disputant is satisfied that you understand his/her point of view and feelings, then each disputant paraphrases what he/she believes the other's point of view and feelings are.
9. When the disputants both agree that the other understand their point of view and feelings, each tells what he/she needs to resolve the problem.
10. Brainstorm and write down all ideas.
11. Evaluate ideas.
12. Agree on a solution.
13. Write and sign an agreement. (Include who, what, when, where, how.)
14. Agree what to tell friends. (Very important!)
15. Congratulate disputants.

Chapter 15

ADVICE FROM HOUSEPARENTS

In the last chapter, we discussed ways of solving conflict. In this chapter, we will share answers to a survey that we sent out to houseparents around the country.

The survey asked supervisors to select the best houseparents they knew to answer the following questions: What is your best piece of advice to new houseparents and how did you come to know it? And what pitfalls would you advise new houseparents to guard against and how did you come to know this?

We want to start this section with a letter from a young housemom, Diane Nestler, from Raleigh, North Carolina. (All other responses will be given anonymously.) Although it is rather lengthy, we think that her advice, given as the description of a houseparent, is so good that it deserves to be reprinted in full. Note that since the houseparents at her institution are called *teaching-parents,* she used that term, and so we have left it the way she wrote it. But you can substitute the word *houseparent* for *teacher* or teaching-parent when you read it. She wrote:

Teacher: coach, guide, counselor, parent, mentor, role model.
Friend: acquaintance, comrade, chum, buddy, sidekick, playmate.

 A child, like a little boat, needs guideposts to keep it headed in the right direction (a coach). It needs a reliable lighthouse to keep it clear of danger (a guide). It needs a life preserver on board for help during rough seas (a counselor). It needs bigger, stronger ships to tell it where it is proven safe (a teacher). It needs to see older, worn boats so it can see that it is possible to survive even the mightiest of storms (a mentor). And it needs an experienced captain who carefully chooses its courses (role model). Once a little boat (a child) has all this, it will have all it needs to safely guide itself. And the boat will become wiser. It will cease to venture with wild abandon; for it will grow comfortable with the help of the lighthouse, the directions of the guideposts, the wisdom of the old, worn boats, the safety of the life preservers, and the protection of the big, strong ships. It will quietly come to realize that these are its true friends.

 Teach not with the underlying objective of being accepted or liked. If you are an effective teacher this will come naturally. When a child is at a point where (placement out of home) is a necessity, it is vital that the teaching-parents take the role of concerned, strong, consistent lighthouses rather than that of friendly little boats. A lighthouse is looked up to and heeded. Little boats would smash each other to bits in the very first storm.

It has become very clear to us through our kids' subtle comments and behaviors that they feel that they only need listen to or respect teaching parents who act like teaching-parents, and not chums. Those that act "friend-like" are treated with the least respect in response to their requests and in overheard kid-to-kid conversations.

Wasn't that great? With that in mind, we will proceed with the good advice that other houseparents had to offer.

Several houseparents said that being consistent was the most important thing that new houseparents should know. Concerning consistency, a houseparent from Texas wrote:

> The first thing we heard when we became homeparents was to be firm, fair, and consistent. To me, the essence of that piece of advice is several things: Be firm—let the child know the expectation and consequence up front, then carry through. If you don't carry through, then you've lied to the child and lost some of his/her respect for you. Be fair—the discipline has to fit the transgression. Example: child talks on phone too long: Take phone privileges away for appropriate time. NOT go to room, etc. Consistent—discipline all kids the same. The kids can spot favoritism immediately and will resent it.

Houseparents at another children's home cautioned that consistency was necessary, but that consistency should occur *within an environment that encourages growth* rather than stagnation.

> Consistency in a structured environment which provides space and individuality with varied and limited working experiences to enable (kids) to provide for themselves once discharged from the child care system is our best advice.
>
> Example: A young man who has been in the system most of his life and returned to the same facility three times describes it this way:
>
> A. On first admission—the facility was a dark bottle with the lid on very tight which gave him no space to move or breathe.
>
> B. Second admission—same facility and administration was two dark bottles on top of each other, lid still tightly on which provided no breathing possibilities, but a little more space to move.
>
> C. Third admission: same facility with new structure and administration—was still two bottles, but they were moved far apart, clear sides, and the lid loosely on which gave him more air to breathe, space to exist and express himself, and vision to see hope for the future.

A pair of houseparents from North Carolina pointed out that being consistent relates not only to carrying out unpleasant discipline tasks but also to carrying through on pleasant discipline tasks: promises to reward children for good behavior. They also add the importance of being good role models.

> Being consistent and a good role model are the most important qualities a houseparent could have to be successful. Being consistent means following through on consequences and promises consistently. For example, if you have promised your child that all B's on a report card would be rewarded with eating out at a favorite restaurant, then that should be done as soon as possible. This way, your child sees that you are honest and invested in his or her success. As an example of following through on consequences, if you have established a curfew for your child and it is broken, then the response-cost setup needs to be followed though with immediately. It is important to note that the consequences should be fair and consistently delivered every time the rule is broken.
>
> Being a good role model is very important because children learn from watching and listening to others in their immediate environment.
>
> We have learned that these qualities are necessities in maintaining a child's behavior. Through our job as teaching-parents, we have seen children become very successful when consistency and good role models become part of their everyday life.

Although consistency was often cited as being important, other houseparents highlighted the need to be flexible. From a 45-year-old housemom:

> My best advice is for houseparents to approach their job with as much flexibility as possible. When your household is the size of twelve to fourteen people, it becomes very hard to always keep everyone on one set schedule. I have found this to be true because during the fourteen years we have been houseparents, we have dealt mostly with teenagers. We encourage our kids to be involved in school and church, and it is a constant juggling act to meet everybody's needs and their time schedules. It is impossible to make all of this work without the ability to bend and the willingness to change our plans and goals of accomplishment for each day.

One smart housemom would temper the notion of consistency with the idea that kids are each unique and have unique needs. She wrote, "RECOGNIZE YOUR KIDS' INDIVIDUAL NEEDS!" Another housemom lent support to this caution to the notion of consistency when she wrote:

> Apply only the pressure needed to change a behavior. Don't give the worst consequences for a minor problem. This allows you some choices. *Some children need more discipline or pressure than others.* Know your children and work with (their particular needs and abilities).

Closely related to the idea of consistency, one houseparent cautioned that "going by the book" is usually the safest route for a houseparent. This houseparent wrote:

> Always read the facility's policy book. Most of the time, it has the answers to most of your questions. If there is anything in the policy book that is different from what you see going on, direct your questions to your supervisor or the houseparents who have been there the longest.
>
> If you follow the policy book, you will always have the support of the administration.... You will not get terminated for what the policy book says.

While several houseparents said that consistency was extremely important, one of them, as well as other houseparents, cautioned against carrying out disciplinary tasks when you are angry.

> Never, ever, discipline a child when you are angry. You can't be fair and the child will respect you and appreciate it if you tell them, "I am too angry to be fair with you right now, give me a half hour to an hour time-out and then we will talk."

A housemom from a Baptist home wrote:

> Always try to remain calm and patient. If everyone is angry or upset, you argue and nothing gets accomplished. This is the most important lesson my boys taught me. I work with the oldest group of boys, 15 to 18 years olds. I wanted them to do what I said, when I said it. If they didn't, I got angry and gave too many consequences. This made the situation worse. I felt so guilty for the way I had handled myself, that I would back off some of the consequences because I had overreacted. They saw this as a major weakness and used it against me. I wasn't giving clear instructions or expectations because I was in a hurry to get things finished or frustrated because they weren't finished, the way I thought they should be. The results were: the child ended up in his room with consequences, the chore or job wasn't finished, and I felt like a failure.
>
> After many confrontations and prayers, I realized that nothing has to be done *NOW!* And if I stay calm, everyone around me is calmer.

This housemom went on to explain that when we set up consequences for behavior ahead of time and the child still chooses the behavior that will result in consequences, then we shouldn't become angry; it was the child's choice. She said that once she came to understand this, her job was less stressful and her boys were happier, too.

A housedad of ten years at a Methodist home in the west wrote of staying in control:

> When dealing with a child, the child needs to know that you are in control. By this, I mean that in a confrontive situation, you need to be as calm as possible. No power struggles or yelling. I almost always ask the child at the end of our conversation, "Does this make sense?" or "Does this seem fair?" This gives the

child a feeling that he has a part or some control in the situation. I try not to preach to a child.

From a Methodist home on the east coast, a housemom wrote:

When I became a teaching-parent in 1988, my first supervisor said, "Never let 'em see you sweat." What this has come to mean for me has been invaluable. No matter how long the day has been, how severe the circumstances are, how silly or unsettling the behaviors, or how unreasonable the request may seem, you must remain calm and objective in order to effectively model and teach appropriate behaviors to others and solve problems. Co-workers, kids, families, caseworkers, teachers, etc., need to see that your positive attitude and enthusiasm never visibly wane, regardless of the situation.

One facet of staying calm is avoiding power struggles. Not surprisingly, a number of houseparents addressed this issue. A couple in their early sixties said it this way:

Don't get into power struggles. When this happens, no one wins. State the facts, then leave, not giving (kids) a chance to argue.

From North Carolina comes this advice:

At all costs, avoid power struggles. Out-of-home placements usually are an indication that somewhere control has slipped from the child, the parent, the caseworker, etc., and as another caregiver, you can be viewed as one more threat to someone's power or authority. Additionally, any struggle for power between staff members is bad for employee morale as well as providing a poor role model for the kids in your care and their families. Remembering that the only behavior you control is your own, always monitoring your own intensity, and maintaining objectivity will keep you focused on the long-term goals (the war) rather than the short-term goals (the battle) and will empower everyone involved in the situation.

A 41-year-old housedad told a story about how he learned not to get in power struggles with kids. He wrote:

Don't get in power struggles with kids, and don't take it personally when they curse you out or yell at you. You are the adult and you have to act like one.
Story: An 18-year-old girl yelled at me while I was confronting another girl, and I yelled back, and she yelled back, etc. If I had just said to her, "This doesn't concern you. Please be quiet," I wouldn't have damaged our relationship. As it was, she lost a great deal of respect for me that day. I would say to new homeparents, "Don't be afraid or too proud or stubborn to say the magic phrase, 'I'm sorry, I messed up.' Kids know you are human." I went to the 18-year-old girl a day later, in front of all her housemates, and got some of her respect back by apologizing to her.

In addition to this fellow, a number of other houseparents wrote about the importance of being able to look a kid in the eye and say, "I goofed." It was interesting that this advice most often came from older houseparents.

From a pair of Texas houseparents aged 59 and 60:

> Don't be afraid to make mistakes. We have discovered that if you make a mistake (and you will), admit it. Kids are glad to see that you are human. This is a good teaching tool for truth and honesty.

From a Methodist home housemom aged 60:

> Never be too proud to tell a kid, "I was wrong," "I goofed," or "I made an error."

Like the housedad above who said not to take it personally when a kid yells at you, a housemom from Arkansas explained:

> Don't take everything personally. These kids are angry and they are directing it at you, but most of the time, you are not the source of the problem. They need someone to hang in there through the bad times and bad feelings. They need someone to be firm and set limits so they can feel a sense of security. For me, 100% of the time, a caring, loving relationship has come from this type of situation.

A pair of houseparents in their late twenties pointed out that houseparents should let kids know that not only is it okay for houseparents to make mistakes but it's okay for kids to make mistakes, too.

> Show the youths that mistakes are okay. Remind them that you don't expect perfection from them, just a best effort.
>
> When we began our job, we both had high expectations of ourselves as well as the youths in our care. We soon learned through diminished relationships with each other and with the youths we worked with that making mistakes was acceptable and also a way to learn. Then the youths felt more comfortable in putting forth honest best efforts in most areas of their lives.

One mistake that new houseparents often make is in trying to take the place of a child's mom or dad. Several houseparents addressed this problem.

A young couple from North Carolina wrote:

> Realizing your role in the lives of the children that you work with in the home is the most important advice we can give to houseparents.... One thing that potentially could hinder the success of the child is to begin a parent-child relationship. The strength of the bond between parents and their biological children is irreplaceable. By becoming the "mom and dad," houseparents could hinder a child from reaching her/his full potential. Children, no matter what their background, resent anyone trying to take the place of their parents....

Said a housemom of fourteen years:

> I feel the worst pitfall we have seen since becoming houseparents is that of trying to become another set of parents to the children in our care. I believe in some cases that naturally happens, and in some cases, it can be a good thing. But houseparents who have children of their own owe it to their children to make sure they know they are special to their parents and that no one else can share that place in their parents' hearts. Most of the children in our care have their own family in one form or another, and they really don't want someone trying to take that place. I believe it is the role of the houseparent to help give guidance, support, security, stable surroundings, and provide the example of a responsible adult.

Other houseparents warned of expecting your residents to be like your own children, or of comparing the residents to your own children. Said a housemom:

> Do not expect these children to be like your own. They have not had the upbringing that you have given your own children. They will not behave in the same manner as your own. Most of them have not had the love and attention that you have given your own children....

A housedad of twenty years warned:

> Do not expect the children you work with to be like your own flesh and blood children. If you "failed" with your own children, there is no way to atone for past failures with other kids. My statement comes from several homeparents who expressed words of this nature.

While houseparents, shouldn't try and take the special place that belongs to a child's mom or dad, and shouldn't expect kids to be like their own children, other houseparents pointed out the fact that kids need to feel loved and nurtured by their houseparents.

Said a couple of veteran houseparents from the south:

> Houseparents: you need to understand why you are in this position. You, as a houseparent, will need to love, respect, trust, and have patience (a lot) with the children you have in your care. A lot of the children we get do not know what it is to be loved, respected, trusted, or have parents who have patience.... A lot of them have been abused in many different ways. Remember, God made each child different, so they need to be treated differently, but all need to be treated fairly and with love.

An older housedad agreed, acknowledging that not every kid who comes into your home will be easy to love. He wrote:

> Do not play favorites. Learn to love even the kids you don't like.

The dangers of being manipulated by kids was the topic of discussion for a number of houseparents. From a houseparent team at a Roman Catholic children's home:

(Guard against) manipulation by residents which they will try to use between houseparents, other staff, and even amongst themselves.... Since young residents have limited means to get what they want...manipulation...(is) the most natural and easiest way of attempting to get what they want. When the team/staff is united, it is strong, and when broken apart, it is weaker....

From a housemom at another institution:

Don't let kids split staff. The girls at (the cottage) would ask me a question, then turn around and ask (the housedad) the same question. We learned to tell the girls that we would have to talk it over with the partner. (The girls) also tell the supply homeparents that the 8-day homeparents let them do certain things that are not true.

A housemom from Michigan put the problem of manipulation this way:

Do not trust these "poor, innocent, abused kids" until they have earned it. They are expert liars, adept at "dividing and conquering" houseparents. I was naive and wanted the kids to like me in the beginning. Now, I look them in the eye and say, "I would like to believe you, but I don't. I hope that some day I can trust your word."

Taking time out before making an important decision was addressed by a husband and wife who have been houseparents for twenty years. Said the husband:

Never make snap judgments. You must take time to think things through and make sure you are under control.

Said the wife:

When you decide to quit or make any major decision, always sleep on it. Things look better the next day. I have probably thought about quitting thousands of times. After I slept on it, I was refreshed and ready to go again.

This same housemom offered other advice-related decision making. She advises houseparents, "Don't sweat the small stuff. Decide what battles are worth fighting for." In my practice as a houseparent (and as a teacher) I have seen adults sweating all kinds of small stuff, fighting battles that simply weren't worth fighting. What does it really matter if Eric won't eat his rhubarb? Chances are that he's getting plenty of other fruits and vegetables in his diet, so he's not going to die of malnutrition. What does it really matter if Sammy didn't take off his Sunday pants before he started playing in the floor of his room? The pants can be washed. It's really no big deal; life is too short to fight about such things.

This same housemom also offered a piece of advice that has been my advice to myself during the worst times of my life. She wrote, "In bad times, remember these immortal words: This, too, shall pass." When I am going through a bad time, I say those words to myself and I visualize a muddy river. I know that I have to cross the river and it will be cold and muddy and unpleasant. But I know that the river is neither swift enough nor deep enough to drown me, so all I have to do is get tough and start across. I can see the other bank and I know that I won't be in the muddy water forever, just until I can get to the other side.

This woman's husband offered advice about understanding and appreciating children. He wrote:

> You have no right to expect great displays of gratitude or affection from the children you work with. With some children, the more you try, the less they appreciate your efforts. Also, realize that there is always some good in the biggest "stinker." Sincerely attempt to use that as a starting point.

Two sets of houseparents cautioned new houseparents against listening to old houseparents who speak negatively of a child you are going to have in your home. Said one couple:

> One of the many things for new houseparents to learn is to not listen to the old houseparents about a child. Learn for yourself about the child. Give the child a chance. You may treat this child differently from the way the other houseparents treated her. That child may be entirely different for you. Love and attention go a long way in the care of a child.
>
> When we first came here, old houseparents told us we were going to get a girl named Jean (not her real name). They told us she was the worst kid on the campus, she had a smart mouth, and we would not be able to get along with her. This girl moved in and lived with us for four years. She graduated from high school and junior college and still calls us and comes to see us. Had we listened to the other houseparents, we may as well have packed up and left. . . . She is just one of many that we have loved and sent on their future course of life.

In a related vein, a houseparent of sixteen years warned against gossip of any kind, whether about kids or other staff. This houseparent wrote:

> Avoid facility gossip. It can tear down positive adult role models and put distance between staff who should be working together. Everyone has something to offer. Most of the time, the gossip gets back to the kids you are working with. They often use this in manipulative ways. Also avoid gossip about the kids between staff.

While gossip is always harmful, a houseparent couple stressed the importance of communication among staff. They wrote:

Open communication between all staff members (is important). The more information you have, the better job you can do to help the kids. Someone may have an idea to solve the problem that you have not thought of. (Open communication helps) stop manipulation. Open communication helps to create team unity.

Many houseparents addressed the problem of burnout. Here are some suggestions that were offered for helping reduce the stress that leads to burnout:

Pace yourself. Know your limits. Don't forget to take care of you. You are very important and if you take care of yourself, you can be a better servant to the children in your care.

Learn to "let go" when you have done all you believe you can do for a child. You can damage a child's chances of making it when you hang on too long. Recommend some change of workers and/or home unit of this person.... Do not blame yourself if a child doesn't make it after you have given your very best. We used to take our failures personally.

When you go on time off, don't take your job with you.

One of the pitfalls of homeparenting is burnout. I try to avoid this by doing the best job I can while on duty and leaving it at the job when I go off duty. Try and remember, you cannot help *every* child. Don't take it personally when a child fails....

In a similar vein, one young housemom stressed the importance of enjoying your job and suggested that spending quality time with the kids was part of enjoying the job.

My best piece of advice for houseparents is to not get caught up in the daily routine ... and find yourself too stressed and fatigued to enjoy your job. As we all know, being responsible for the well-being of the children, laundry, food preparation, administration of medication, transportation, and daily paperwork can be draining at times. TAKE TIME OUT TO SPEND WITH THE CHILDREN. Engage in activities or watch movies together. This time can be beneficial to you as a caretaker, and it also allows the children an opportunity to observe you in a relaxed state. By participating in activities with children, you also have the opportunity to engage in conversations that are not filled with instructions, reprimands, and negative connotations. You have shared an experience or memory that is fun and relaxing which can be reflected on in times of stress.... You will probably find that by spending more time with the children that they appreciate and respect you more than if you are consistently too busy with daily routines to pay attention to their needs.... ENJOY YOUR JOB AS A TEMPORARY PARENT!

One housemom wanted new houseparents to know that it's important to trust your instincts or your intuitive ways of knowing. And also to be forgiving. She wrote:

> Give one more chance when your head tells you different... trust your gut feeling.
>
> José had been doing well... his older brother had completed our program, and José himself had been with us four months. He fell under the influence of a foster brother who led him down the "wrong road." They stole our car and crashed it when the police chased them. Upon visiting José in the detention center, he was remorseful. He wrote a letter committing never to hurt us again. Eight months later, he graduated our program, having kept his word. Our heads said, "Don't take him back," but we're glad we followed our hearts. He's still in touch with us after three years and doing well.

Finally, several houseparents told us that their religious faith was central to their advice to houseparents. From Alabama comes this advice:

> I think that this work is the greatest work possible. The first thing is to have a *calling within self,* knowing that this is one of the most important things in a child's life. In the training of good houseparents, Number 1 is personal integrity. Number 2, self-control. Number 3, honesty. Number 4, the ability to listen. Number 5, a love for others and God.

Last but not least, a housemom from Missouri wrote:

> The best piece of advice for Direct Care Providers is, first of all, to pray for guidance and direction.

While it may not be important for many people, for me, when I was a houseparent, my religious faith and the belief that I had been called to that type of service for that period of time was essential in helping me get through my day-to-day battles. A personnel director of a large, well-known children's home told me once that the most important quality he could think of in a houseparent was "a missionary's heart." "If you've got that," he said, "the rest comes easy."

In this chapter, we have shared the responses that houseparents from across the country gave us on our questionnaires about best advice. In the next chapter, we will discuss techniques of coping with stress so you can better prevent burnout.

Chapter 16

HANDLING STRESS

In the last chapter, we shared the advice offered by houseparents around the country. In this chapter, we want to discuss stress and ways you can learn to handle it more successfully.

If you're going to spend your life raising other people's kids, you're going to have stress. Of course, you're going to have stress in your life even if you are in some other line of work, too. But living with a dozen or so kids, and often another set of adults, is going to present you with more stress than many other occupations.

Stress has been defined in a number of ways. One definition is from the pioneer stress researcher, Hans Selye. Selye defined stress as "the nonspecific response of the body to any demand made upon it." Things which produce stress for us are called *stressors*. The way we respond to stressors is called *stress reactivity*. Our stress reactivity can be thought of as our fight-or-flight reaction.

It's not just the bad things that happen to us that are stressful; the good things that happen to us are stressful, too. We call good-thing stress *eustress*, while the bad-thing stress is called *distress*. But whether it's good stress or bad stress, the effects on our bodies are the same.

Whether from good or bad stress, our bodies respond by pumping out hormones and chemicals. Among the chemicals and hormones we produce during times of stress are cortisol and aldosterone. Cortisol is what provides the fuel for our fight or flight. Cortisol increases the blood sugar in our system so we'll be able to bound across the meadow or punch out the lights of the lion that's chasing us. It also breaks down protein in our bodies and increases our blood pressure. Another function of cortisol is to decrease the number of lymphocytes in our bodies. Lymphocytes kill germs that get into our bodies, so a reduction in lymphocytes means that our immune system is decreased and we are more likely to get sick.

The purpose of aldosterone is to prepare us for fight or flight. It increases blood pressure, decreases our urine output, and makes us retain salt.

Other chemicals are released in our bodies, too. Adrenalin and noradrenalin are also produced. These hormones make our heart beat faster and harder, open up our bronchial tubes in our lungs, and constrict the blood vessels in our muscles and skin. It also speeds up our normal body processes.

Thyroxin is another hormone that is released during stress. In addition to helping the other responses we've named, thyroxin also speeds up our gastrointestinal system. This often results in our having diarrhea. Thyroxin also increases our feelings of anxiety and gives us energy.

Now all these hormones and their effects are invaluable if we need to run for our lives from a saber-toothed tiger or even a hoodlum who is chasing us. This stress reactivity is what helps us run fast and jump high and escape with our lives. The problem is that we are rarely reacting to the stressor of a saber-toothed tiger or a hoodlum. Most of our stressors are social or psychological. Our supervisor chewed us out. Some other people's kid smarted off to us. Our relief houseparent didn't do things the way we wanted them done. These stressors produce the very same physiological responses we need to fight or flee. But punching out our supervisor or running willy-nilly down the road aren't solutions to our problems, so all of these hormones build up in our bodies and eventually make us sick.

Hans Selye explained that stress reactivity has three stages. The first phase is called the *alarm reaction stage*. This is characterized by the onset of the processes we addressed above. The second phase is called the *stage of resistance*. If we can adapt to the stressor, the signs of the flight-or-fight symptoms tend to disappear and our resistance rises above normal levels. However, if the stressor does not go away, we will eventually enter the third phase, the *stage of exhaustion*. In extreme cases, the body eventually expends all of its energy. The signs of alarm reappear, but now they are irreversible, and the person dies.

Stress can lead to illness. We can probably all point to times when we were sick following a time of protracted stress. These stress-induced illnesses include heart attack, stroke, cancer, rheumatoid arthritis, headaches, and backaches, as well as other diseases. Our bodies wear out while we're fighting the stress and we become susceptible to serious illness. Our bodies also produce hormones which actually promote illnesses. For example, stress helps *create* the plaque that can line blood vessels and result in either heart attack or stroke.

Two important ways of reducing stress include having good communication skills and good conflict resolution skills, which we discussed earlier in the book. Another way of reducing stress is asserting yourself. Assertiveness can be thought of as being able to satisfy your own needs and to express yourself. You should be able to feel good about being assertive. The difference between assertive and aggressive behavior is that when you are assertive, you do not hurt others in the process of meeting your own needs. When you are aggressive, you will hurt others in order to meet your needs. So be assertive, not aggressive.

Another way of reducing stress is to set goals, write them down, prioritize them, and then carry them out. Having something important that you have to do looming over your head is a great stressor. Identifying it and tackling it is seldom as hard as worrying about having to do it.

Humor is a great stress reducer. Try and find something humorous in every situation. Finding a way to make yourself laugh will produce hormones that combat the stress hormones. Be sure and take time out to watch your favorite comedy on TV. Consider it time invested in your personal well-being.

In their book, *Type A Behavior and Your Heart*, Friedman and Rosenman, offer a number of suggestions for reducing stress. One of the ones we like most is to "Remember that life is always an unfinishedness." They explain that thinking that once you finish everything that you currently need to do, you will be finished, is counterproductive to health. As soon as you finish everything on your to-do list, a whole new list of things that you have to do will appear like magic. So once you realize that the things you have to do will never be finished, you can begin to reduce your stress.

Jerrold S. Greenberg, in his wonderful book, *Coping with Stress: A Practical Guide*, explains that realizing that you have a good deal of control over what happens in your life is a great stress-fighter. Such a realization is called having an *internal locus of control*. However, it's not healthy to think that you can control *everything* in your life. On the extreme end of the continuum would be the internal locus of control people who believe that they can control everything in their lives. In contrast, Greenberg explains that people with an *external locus of control* believe that they have *no* control over what happens in their lives. Neither of these positions is healthy.

The healthy position is realizing that there are some things in your life that you cannot control, but there are many things that you can control. Perhaps that brings us to the serenity prayer: Lord, grant me the serenity to accept the things I cannot change, courage to change the things I can, and wisdom to know the difference. We suspect that that prayer has been a great source of comfort for many a person who is raising other people's kids.

Another stress-fighting technique is called *self-talk*. You will remember from our chapter on learning that Vygotsky explains that we engage in self-talk naturally whenever we are working on a task that we haven't fossilized yet. Much of our self-talk may be related to stressful situations, and we may use it to make ourselves even more stressed out.

One of my graduate students, Gloria Burdine, was interested in self-talk and wanted to see if she could change negative self-talk that at-risk teenagers use on themselves. She planned an experiment in which she had three counseling sessions with at-risk teens which would teach them to engage in positive self-talk. On the day that her experiment was to begin, she had someone send a note to each of the teens to come to the school office. After they arrived, she asked the teens what they were telling themselves on the way to the office. Every one of the teenagers was telling herself that she was in trouble. Gloria worked with the teens and found good results in teaching them to engage in positive self-talk.

Closely related to self-talk is a technique that Greenberg calls *re-labeling* but my Aunt Doris calls "looking for the good in people" and situations. When I was a little kid, Aunt Doris told me that she always tried to find the good in people and concentrate on that, rather than on the bad in them. She said that sometimes it was a challenge to find the good in someone, but that if I would look closely enough, I could find it. I've tried hard to do that and have generally been successful. When you can find the good in someone and concentrate on it, then it is less stressful to have to deal with them. Try it and see if it doesn't work for you.

Next, we want to talk about relaxation techniques. Since stress speeds up your heart, raises your blood pressure, increases your gastric juices and serum cholesterol and other such things, learning to relax your body and combat stress is invaluable. However, before beginning any stress-reduction program, you should consult your doctor. If, for example, you are on medication, then it may be that engaging in stress-reduction techniques would require a change in your dosage. So be on the safe side and consult your doctor before you start on any relaxation program.

One technique for relaxation and reducing the body's stress reactivity is meditation. Although meditation has its roots in such places as Tibet and India, many westerners have adopted it. Meditation does not require that a person adopt a certain religion in order to practice it. You can be a good Baptist or Catholic or Jew and still practice meditation. All meditation is a kind of focusing the attention or opening up the attention in order to reach a state of relaxation.

Meditation has been documented to slow breathing and heart rate, to change the skin's galvanic response (ability to conduct electrical current), and to increase the production of alpha brain waves. Masters of this art have been scientifically documented to slow their breathing to four to six breaths per minute and to slow their heart rate by twenty-four beats per minute. Meditation has also been proven to lower the lactate levels in the blood, improve sleep, and relieve headaches.

Here is one way to meditate: Sit in a comfortable chair. Don't lie down, or you will probably fall asleep. While you can meditate yourself to sleep if you want to, you won't receive the benefits of meditation if you do fall asleep. So sit in a comfortable chair. Sit straight up and relax your hands either on your lap or on the arms of the chair. Close your eyes and relax. Don't work at relaxing, because that's work. Simply relax as best as you can without working at it.

After you have relaxed for a moment, begin to count in your mind, "One," each time you inhale and "Two," each time you exhale, or "In," and "Out," or some other emotionally neutral syllable. Keep your breathing relaxed and natural and continue for twenty minutes.

You will catch yourself thinking thoughts until you become quite experienced at meditation. When you catch yourself thinking, don't blame yourself or feel bad. All novice meditators catch themselves thinking while they are supposed to be meditating. Simply go back to focusing on your breathing and resume meditating.

You can check your watch when you think your twenty minutes are up, but don't set an alarm. The alarm will ruin your relaxed state.

After the meditation session is over, open your eyes, take several deep breaths, stretch, and slowly stand up. You must stand up slowly, because your blood pressure should have been lowered and you may be a little dizzy when you stand up.

Another form of relaxation is called *progressive relaxation*. Progressive relaxation (also called *Jacobsonian relaxation*) was developed by a medical doctor named Edmund Jacobsen. In his book (called *Progressive Relaxation*), Jacobsen explains the technique, which combats *bracing*. Bracing is the term used when muscles are tensed unconsciously and unnecessarily. When sitting at my computer, I sometimes notice that the muscles in my neck, back, and shoulders are tensed. Often when I am lying in bed unable to sleep, I notice that my entire body is tensed. When driving in the car, I often notice that my brow is furrowed and my neck is rigid. These are examples of bracing.

In order to practice progressive relaxation, remove your shoes and any tight clothing. Lie on the floor with a small pillow under your neck and, if you wish, under the back of your knees. Then, starting with your right foot, alternately tense and relax your muscles. Pay attention to how it feels when the muscles are tensed. Then pay attention to how it feels when the muscles are relaxed. Repeat the tensing and relaxing, paying close attention to how each feels. Repeat the procedure with your left foot. Then proceed to move up your body to the muscles in the calf of your right leg. Continue until you finish with the muscles in your scalp. Conduct progressive relaxation exercises three times a day for five minutes and you should begin to see positive results in a short period of time. There are a number of related methods of progressive relaxation which you can learn by borrowing a book from your local library.

Exercise is one of the best methods of combatting stress. Since stress reactivity prepares us to fight or flee, a good workout efficiently expends the hormones that are pumped into our body. After all, our bodies can't tell whether we're running from a saber-toothed tiger or in a big circle around the gym. The effects are the same. Again, please consult your physician before beginning any exercise program.

In this chapter, we have shared with you some techniques for reducing stress. We talked about some stress-prevention measures, such as setting goals, prioritizing them, and tackling them, instead of worrying about them. We also talked about some relaxation techniques which may help you combat the stress that you can't prevent.

We hope that you will use these and other techniques to handle stress, because houseparent/caregiver burnout may be the most serious problem in the child care business. Without folks like you, folks who are willing to invest their all into raising other people's kids, the world would be a lot worse off. You are the folks who want to make the world a better place. You are the folks who take a bad situation and make it better. You are the folks who wrap your arms around a hopeless child and give her hope. There can't be any higher calling.

INDEX

A

Abstract thought (*see* Formal operational thought)
Accommodation, 17–19
Adaptation, 19
Adolescent egocentricism, 62–63
Adrenalin, 167
Alarm reaction stage, 167
Aldosterone, 166
Alpha wolf, 82
Animism, 15
Arbitrator, 145
Assimilation, 17
Authoritarian parenting style, 114–115
Authoritative parenting style, 115
Autonomy vs. shame and doubt, 48

B

Behavior problems, 105–106
Bracing, 170–171

C

Career, 57–58
Clearly defined limits, 69
Collective monologue, 15
Communication skills, 128–141
Concrete operational thought, 7, 17–22
Conflict, 142
Conservation tasks, 13
Constraints, 86, 92
Conventional morality, 26–31
Cooperative work and helping relations, 38, 42–43
Corporal punishment (*see* Punishment, Cortisol, 166)

D

Decentration, 21
Deferred imitation, 11
Defossilization, 99, 101
Direct vs. indirect communication style, 138
Discipline, 105–116
Disequilibration, 20
Dispositional thinking, 61
Distress, 166
Dominance gradient, 83

E

Effort, 91
Egocentrism, 12, 14
Elaborate vs. succinct communication style, 139–140
Embarrassment, 28–31
Empathic listening, 136–137, 140
Empathy, 134–137
Epigenesis, 6–7
Equilibration, 20
Eustress, 166
Exercise, 171
Exogeneous skeleton, 57
Extending language, 10
Extrinsic motivation, 84–86

F

Finalism, 15
Formal operational thought, 7, 22–24
Fossilization, 99, 101
Freedom, 79, 84, 106
From goodness to truth, 34–35
From selfishness to responsibility, 33
Fun, 79, 81, 87, 106

G

Generativity vs. stagnation, 53
Gestures, 130–132
Good boy/nice girl stage (*see* Interpersonal conformity orientation)
Guaranteed success, 92

H

Haptics, 129–130

I

I-messages, 146–148
Identity achievement, 58–59
Identity crisis, 54–65
Identity diffusion, 58–60
Identity foreclosure, 58–59
Identity moratorium, 58–59
Identity vs. identity diffusion, 52
Imaginary audience, 62–63
Imitation, 8–10
Immaculate perception, 16
Immune system, 166
Individual survival, 33
Industry vs. inferiority, 51–52
Initiative vs. guilt, 50
Instrumental exchange orientation, 27
Instrumental vs. affective communication style, 141
Integrity vs. despair, 53
Intellectual development, 7–24
Interpersonal conformity orientation, 27–28
Intimate space, 117–118
Intimacy vs. isolation, 52–53
Intrinsic motivation, 84
Irreversibility, 12, 14

J

Jacobsonian relaxation (*see* Progressive relaxation)

L

Law and order orientation, 31
Learned helplessness, 90–92
Levels of assistance, 102–104

Locus of control, 168
Lymphocytes, 166

M

Magical thinking, 11
Marasmus, 70
Meditation, 169–170
Mediator, 145
Minimax strategy, 86–87
Moral development, 25–44
Moral dilemmas, 25–26
Morality of caring, 24, 33–37
Morality of justice, 25–32
Morality of nonviolence, 35–36
Motivation, 79–94
Multiple classifications, 21–22

N

Need to belong, 80–81, 106
NVC (*see* Nonverbal communication)
Nonverbal communication, 128–132
Noradrenalin, 167

O

Object permanence, 8–9

P

Participation in decision-making, 38, 44, 89
Perceptual centration, 12–14
Permissive parenting style, 115
Personal space, 118–119
Perspectivistic thinking, 61–62
Personal fable, 62–63
Parental warmth, 69–70
Pleasure-pain level (*see* Punishment-obedience level)
Preconventional morality, 26–27
Prior rights and social contract orientation, 32
Postconventional morality, 26
Power, 79, 81–82, 89, 106–107
Preoperational thought, 7, 11
Progressive relaxation, 170–171
Proxemics, 117–125
Public space, 120

Punishment, 107–114
Punishment-obedience level, 26–27, 70
Psychosocial development, 45–53, 54–65
Psychosocial moratorium, 58

R

Reflection upon moral issues, 38, 43–44
Re-labeling, 169
Relaxation techniques, 169–171
Respectful treatment, 69
Restitution, 106–107
Retribution, 106–107
Reversibility, 20
Risk of failure, 92
Role taking, 61–62
Rules and procedures for mediating conflict resolution, 149–154

S

Scaffolding, 101–102
Schema, 17–20
Schemata, 17–20
Self-concept, 66
Self-esteem, 38–42, 66–78
Self-evaluation, 66–68
Self-sacrifice and social conformity, 33–34
Self talk, 169
Self-worth, 66–67
Sense of social community, 38, 41–42
Sensorimotor development, 7
Sexuality, 55, 79–80
Shame, 51

Social space, 120
Socially Mediated Apprenticeship Theory, 97–101
Sociopaths, 70
Spanking (*see* Punishment)
Speech convergence, 133–134
Speech divergence, 133
Stage of resistance, 167
Stage of exhaustion, 167
Stress, 166–171
Stressors, 166
Stress reactivity, 166
Survival and reproduction needs, 79–80, 106
Symbolic representation, 12

T

Thyroxin, 167
Trust vs. mistrust, 47–48

U

Undermining effect, 86
Universal ethical principles orientation, 32

W

Wisdom, 53
Worst kid syndrome, 126

Z

Zone of proximal development, 98, 101
ZPD (*see* Zone of proximal development)

CHARLES C THOMAS • PUBLISHER, LTD.

- Johnson, Donald D.—**DEAFNESS AND VISION DISORDERS: Anatomy and Physiology, Assessment Procedures, Ocular Anomalies, and Educational Implications.** '99, 500 pp. (6 3/4 x 9 3/4), 29 il. (15 in color), 76 tables.

- Jewell, David L.—**CONFRONTING CHILD MALTREATMENT THROUGH RECREATION. (2nd Ed.)** '99, 376 pp. (7 x 10), 1 il., 28 tables.

- Mitchell, Juliann W.—**THE DYNAMICS OF CRISIS INTERVENTION: Loss as the Common Denominator.** '98, 270 pp. (7 x 10).

- Kronick, Robert F. & Charles Hargis—**DROP-OUTS: Who Drops Out and Why - and the Recommended Action. (2nd Ed.)** '98, 224 pp. (7 x 10), 3 il., $34.95, paper.

- Roberts, Albert R.—**SOCIAL WORK IN JUVENILE AND CRIMINAL JUSTICE SETTINGS. (2nd Ed.)** 97, 474 pp. (7 x 10), 1 il., 16 tables, $87.95, cloth, $69.95, paper.

- Walsh, William M. & G. Robert Williams—**SCHOOLS AND FAMILY THERAPY: Using Systems Theory and Family Therapy in the Resolution of School Problems.** '97, 236 pp. (7 x 10), 2 il., 5 tables, $47.95, cloth, $34.95, paper.

- Kelly, Francis D.—**THE CLINICAL INTERVIEW OF THE ADOLESCENT: From Assessment and Formulation to Treatment Planning.** '97, 234 pp. (7 x 10), 2 tables, $59.95, cloth $45.95, paper

- Harrison, Dianne F., John S. Wodarski & Bruce A. Thyer—**CULTURAL DIVERSITY AND SOCIAL WORK PRACTICE. (2nd Ed.)** '96, 360 pp. (7 x 10), 2 tables, $70.95, cloth, $48.95, paper.

- Fine, Aubrey H. & Nya M. Fine—**THERAPEUTIC RECREATION FOR EXCEPTIONAL CHILDREN: Let Me In, I Want to Play. (2nd Ed.)** 96, 422 pp. (7 x 10), 17 il, $73.95, cloth, $52.95, paper.

- Ballew, Julius R. & George Mink—**CASE MANAGEMENT IN SOCIAL WORK: Developing the Professional Skills Needed for Work with Multiproblem Clients. (2nd Ed.)** '96, 334 pp. (7 x 10), 23 il, $55.95, cloth, $41.95, paper.

- Royse, David—**HOW DO I KNOW IT'S ABUSE? Identifying and Countering Emotional Mistreatment from Friends and Family Members.** '94, 248 pp. (7 x 10), $54.95, cloth, $37.95, paper.

- Freeman, Edith M. & Marianne Pennekamp—**SOCIAL WORK PRACTICE: Toward a Child, Family, School, Community Perspective.** '88, 354 pp. (7 x10), 4 il., 2 tables, $58.95, cloth, $38.95, paper.

- Lungu, Karen L.—**CHILDREN WITH SPECIAL NEEDS: A Resource Guide for Parents, Educators, Social Workers, and Other Caregivers.** '99, 234 pp. (7 x 10).

- Bryan, Willie V.—**MULTICULTURAL ASPECTS OF DISABILITIES: A Guide to Understanding and Assisting Minorities in the Rehabilitation Process.** '99, 246 pp. (7 x 10), 19 tables.

- Greenberg, Samuel I.—**INTRODUCTION TO THE TECHNIQUE OF PSYCHOTHERAPY: Practice Guidelines for Psychotherapists.** '98, 122 pp. (7 x 10), 1 table, $32.95, cloth, $ 20.95, paper.

- Gray, David E.—**AUTISM AND THE FAMILY: Problems, Prospects, and Coping with the Disorder.** '98, 210 pp. (7 x 10), 4 tables, $45.95, cloth, $32.95, paper.

- Thorman, George—**FAMILY THERAPY: A Social Work Approach.** '97, 150 pp. (7 x 10), 7 il., $44.95, cloth, $29.95, paper.

- Forst, Martin L.—**THE POLICE AND THE HOMELESS: Creating a Partnership Between Law Enforcement and Social Service Agencies in the Development of Effective Policies and Programs.** '97, 248 pp. (7 x 10), 1 il., 7 tables, $57.95, cloth, $42.95, paper.

- France, Kenneth—**CRISIS INTERVENTION: A Handbook of Immediate Person-to-Person Help. (3rd Ed.)** '96, 310 pp. (7 x 10), 3 il., $52.95, cloth, $36.95, paper.

- Hendricks, James E. & Bryan Byers—**CRISIS INTERVENTION IN CRIMINAL JUSTICE/SOCIAL SERVICE. (2nd Ed.)** '96, 430 pp. (7 x 10), 7 tables, $75.95, cloth, $54.95, paper.

- Moon, Bruce L.—**ART AND SOUL: Reflections on an Artistic Psychology.** '96, 156 pp. (7 x 10), 15 il., $36.95, cloth, $25.95, paper.

- Phillips, Norma Kolko & S. Lala Ashenberg Straussner—**CHILDREN IN THE URBAN ENVIRONMENT: Linking Social Policy and Clinical Practice.** '96, 258 pp. (7 x 10), 2 il., 1 table, $60.95, cloth, $46.95, paper.

- Locke, Shirley A.—**COPING WITH LOSS: A GUIDE FOR CAREGIVERS.** '94, 238 pp. (7 x 10), $51.95, cloth, $35.95, paper.

- Mayers, Raymond Sanchez, Barbara L. Kail & Thomas D. Watts—**HISPANIC SUBSTANCE ABUSE.** '93, 258 pp. (7 x 10), 3 il., 9 tables, $54.95, cloth, $37.95, paper.

- Thompson, Richard H. & Gene Stanford—**CHILD LIFE IN HOSPITALS: Theory and Practice.** '81, 284 pp., 1 table, $40.95, paper.

Call 1-800-258-8980 or 1-217-789-8980 or FAX (217)789-9130 • www.ccthomas.com • books@ccthomas.com
Books sent on approval • Shipping charges: $5.50 U.S. / $6.50 Canada • Prices subject to change without notice

2600 South First Street • Springfield • Illinois • 62704

DOWNTOWN CAMPUS LRC

J. SARGEANT REYNOLDS COMMUNITY COLLEGE

3 7219 00114900 7

```
HQ 767.9 .C353 1995
Camerer, M. C. Gore
Raising other people's kids
```

DISCARDED

**J. SARGEANT REYNOLDS
COMMUNITY COLLEGE**
Richmond, VA